Reading for Understanding

Reading for Understanding

A Guide to
Improving Reading
in Middle and High
School Classrooms

Ruth Schoenbach • Cynthia Greenleaf • Christine Cziko • Lori Hurwitz

Published in Partnership with WestEd

JOSSEY-BASS
A Wiley Company
San Francisco

Grateful acknowledgment is made for permission to reprint the following:

Epigraph in Chapter 1 from "Exploring Reading Nightmares of Middle and Secondary School Teachers" by W. P. Bintz from *Journal of Adolescent and Adult Literacy*, 1997, 40(1), 12-24. Reprinted with permission of International Reading Association.

"Kevin Clarke" reproduced with permission of Nadine Rosenthal. In *Speaking of Reading* (Heinemann, A division of Reed Elsevier Inc., Portsmouth, NH, 1995).

"George Ishmael" reproduced with permission of Nadine Rosenthal. In *Speaking of Reading* (Heinemann, A division of Reed Elsevier Inc., Portsmouth, NH, 1995).

"Attention: Keeping the Body and Mind in Control" (Figure 4.1) from *Keeping a Head in School: A Student's Book About Learning Abilities and Learning Disorders* by M. Levine. Reprinted with permission of Educator's Publishing Services.

Excerpts (in Exhibit 5.2) from *Bless Me, Ultima*. Copyright © Rudolfo Anaya 1974. Published in hardcover and mass market paperback by Warner Books Inc. 1994; originally published by TQS Publications. Reprinted by permission of Susan Bergholz Literary Services, New York. All rights reserved.

"Teaching the Think-Aloud Process" exercise in Chapter 5 adapted from *Reading Strategies and Practices: A Compendium,* 5th ed., by Robert J. Tierney and John E. Readance. Copyright © 2000 by Allyn & Bacon. Adapted by permission.

"Totalitarianism Turned Hate into Genocide" from *World History: Perspectives on the Past—Issues of the Modern Age* by Larry S. Krieger and Kenneth Neill. Copyright © 1997 by D. C. Heath and Company. All rights reserved. Reprinted with permission of McDougal Littell Inc.

Excerpts of "The Catbird Seat" from the book *The Thurber Carnival* Copyright © 1945 by James Thurber. Copyright renewed 1972 by Helen Thurber and Rosemary A. Thurber. Reprinted by arrangement with Rosemary A. Thurber and the Barbara Hogenson Agency.

Manufactured in the United States of America.

Library of Congress Cataloging-in-Publication Data

Reading for understanding : a guide to improving reading in middle and high school classrooms / Ruth Schoenbach . . . [et al.].— 1st ed.
    p. cm. — (The Jossey-Bass education series)
  Includes bibliographical references.
  ISBN 0-7879-5045-9 (pbk. : alk. paper)
  1. Reading (Secondary)—United States. 2. Reading (Middle school)—United States. I. Schoenbach, Ruth. II. Series.
LB1632 .R357 2000
428.4'071'2—dc21
                                            99-006978

PB Printing   10 9 8 7 6 5   FIRST EDITION

The Jossey-Bass Education Series

Contents

Foreword   xi
     P. David Pearson

Preface   xv

Acknowledgments   xix

The Sponsor   xxiii

The Authors   xxv

PART ONE: CONFRONTING THE PROBLEM OF MIDDLE AND HIGH SCHOOL READING

1   Rethinking the Problem: Crisis and Opportunity   3

2   The Reading Apprenticeship Framework   17

PART TWO: READING APPRENTICESHIP IN THE CLASSROOM

3   Developing Academic Literacy   45

4   Motivating Students to Take Control of Their Reading   54

5   Acquiring Cognitive Tools for Reading   74

6   Building Context, Text, and Disciplinary Knowledge   99

7   Embedding Apprenticeship Strategies in Subject Area Classrooms   117

8   Overcoming Obstacles in Implementation   138

PART THREE: BEYOND THE CLASSROOM

9   Professional Development: Creating Communities of Master Readers   151

10   Developing Schoolwide Reading Apprenticeship Programs   169

Epilogue: Inviting Continuing Conversation   179

Appendix A: Academic Literacy Curriculum   181

Appendix B: Reading Assessment   187

*To the teachers whose creativity and
commitment continues to inspire and enrich our work*

Foreword

I became aware of the effort detailed in this book some three or four years ago when one of the authors, Ruth Schoenbach, and I were serving on a National Academy of Science (NAS) committee together. I soon learned that Ruth and I shared an interest in literacy—in particular the question of how you work with poor, urban youth to convince them that reading is a worthwhile endeavor. As you can imagine, if you have sneaked a peek at any of the chapters of the book, Ruth's enthusiasm for this work quickly turned the conversation to the Academic Literacy course that, at that time, had just gone through its first full year of implementation and systematic evaluation. I was impressed by what I heard from Ruth in these early conversations—impressed enough to ask for copies of the evaluation reports by Cynthia Greenleaf and descriptions of the program.

At one meeting of our NAS committee, Ruth brought videos of interviews with students; the videos were part of the cases used in training. At another meeting she shared an early draft of a proposal for additional funding, and before I knew it I was hooked. I had become an ardent fan of Academic Literacy, reading apprenticeships, and the professional development network that supported both. Another year passed; Ruth and her colleagues received a grant to expand their Strategic Literacy Network, and I became an adviser to the project.

In my role as an external adviser, I receive updates about every six months and meet with the staff to discuss implementation, research design, and evaluation methods. I also receive regular missives from Ruth or Cynthia about what is going on in the project. So when I was asked to review the manuscript for this book and later to write a foreword for it, there was no question in my mind that I would do so enthusiastically, with great conviction about the importance of the work and great respect for the authors and the network of teachers and the scores of students with and from whom they learn.

My enthusiasm for this effort is grounded in both research and instruction. On the research pole, I admire the way in which the authors and the teachers in the network use reading research to craft their practices. They read the research respectfully and thoroughly, discuss it, consider its utility, and then build and test their own adaptations for their own classrooms and schools. They do what all pedagogical researchers hope teachers will do with their work—take it seriously. In the case of this network, they have taken seriously much of the important work in comprehension of the last twenty years. Their work is well grounded in schema theory, sociocultural theories of learning and literacy, metacognition, cognitive apprenticeships, and a range of comprehension strategies.

For example, the authors write knowledgeably about the importance of connecting the known (what is in your head) to the new (what is there waiting for discovery in the world of text) and enact it by encouraging students to make predictions based on partial information and understanding and by helping students traverse the cognitive demands of different sorts of questions. They cut to the heart of the research on metacognition by modeling for both teachers and students how to make their thinking public so that classroom community members can learn to benefit from one another's difficulties and insights. They make the apprenticeship the heart of their instructional model. Teachers learn how to think, talk, and act the role of a master reader—a reader who can reason her way through the toughest and most obscure of texts. And when the teachers are ready, they invite students to apprentice with them to develop identities as competent and confident readers who are willing to persist in difficult situations.

The pole of practice is equally as well developed in their work. First and foremost, the authors provide sound pedagogical advice for teachers to use with students. The activities, routines, and instructional frameworks are based on valid theoretical constructs, extensive classroom tryout-revision cycles, and hard-nosed evaluation studies. Second, they provide good ideas for staff developers to use in working with groups of teachers. One can surely see in their professional development activities the gentle but firm hand of the National Writing Project. Just as the pedagogy for Writing Project teachers begins with discovering the agonies and ecstasies of being a writer, so the Strategic Literacy Network activities begin with discovering the agonies and ecstasies of being a committed reader. The process engagement, introspection, reflection, metacognition, and public sharing of cognitive secrets all parallel writing process pedagogy for teachers.

Lest you think I discovered this on my own, I must confess that Christine Cziko, one of the authors and designers of the Academic Literacy course, shared her discovery of this parallelism between process writing and, if you will, process reading in a conversation during one of my advisory meetings with the team.

Perhaps the aspect of instruction that most appeals to me is the authors' understanding that forcing teachers to make choices between teaching approaches that, on the surface, seem contradictory actually limits their choices unnecessarily. So, for example, these authors do not take sides between authenticity of text and task at one end of an instructional continuum and ambitious, explicit instruction at the other end. Instead they transform the apparent contradiction into a sort of resonant complementarity, showing that these two seemingly opposite notions actually support one another quite remarkably. In a policy world in which forced choices have become all too common, it is refreshing to see contradictions transformed into synergies.

Finally, let me commend this book to you for an entirely different reason—it is a good read. This book has good ideas, a strong voice, and the clear presence of its teacher audience, standing just out of our view as we read. But enough from me. It is time to hear from the authors.

P. David Pearson
East Lansing, Michigan

Into the Heart of Reading

In a back room off the school library, a boisterous group of ninth-grade students talk about a newly developed yearlong course called Academic Literacy. They started the course in September, and it is now early December. We have asked these students to discuss their impressions so far. They are eager to talk.

LaKeisha starts, describing the new way she thinks about reading. "When you read," she says, "there should be a little voice in your head like a storyteller is saying it. If it's not there, then you're just lookin' at the words." Other students jump in, competing to be heard. They agree they are reading more than they used to. They talk about knowing what kinds of books they like and how to choose a book.

Michael leans back in his chair, arms crossed, and tosses out a mock complaint about his teacher: "Man, she's tryin' to be sneaky! She wants you to pick a book that you are interested in so you will read it more. That's like, what hooks you into reading. . . . She makes you find a book that you *like* so you have to read it. Because you like it."

The talk shifts from choosing books to reading what they "have to" read for their classes. Jason speaks up about a history text he has been reading. "I understand the book more now," he says. "Before, it didn't make sense to me." When asked why he thinks he understands more of his book now, he answers, "Because I read differently now. Like when you're reading, if it doesn't make sense, you can try to restate it in your own words, or you can make questions so you can understand it better. Now I read in between the lines. I basically get into the story, into the heart of it— like reading deeper into what it is saying." Others rush to agree.

The meeting ends forty-five minutes later with cookies and sodas for the students and, for us, a growing sense of excitement. We wonder what will happen as these young men and women become increasingly effective in their reading and begin to add to their self-images the dimension of *successful reader.* We know that one school year cannot reverse lifelong habits and attitudes about reading, and we realize that we have to continue to nurture this fragile growth. But we also believe in the resiliency and resources that adolescents bring to any challenge they are really determined to meet. We leave the room feeling optimistic about the academic future of these blossoming adolescent readers.

Why We Wrote This Book

The authors of this book are two classroom teachers and two senior staff members of a research and professional development project called the Strategic Literacy Initiative (SLI). We decided to write this book to explain how a number of urban adolescents have come to understand reading in new ways. We describe what is happening in dozens of middle and high school classrooms in which we and other teacher colleagues are working to implement a *reading apprenticeship* approach to literacy instruction. Our goal is to help secondary students become engaged, fluent, and competent readers of both academic and recreational texts. We want to invite teachers, school administrators, teacher researchers, and others to join us in this effort.

In this book, we

- Provide a framework for thinking about teaching reading that is clear, powerful, and adaptable across the middle and high school curriculum.

- Provide middle and high school teachers with concrete descriptions of the key ideas and practices of a reading apprenticeship approach in a variety of real classrooms.

- Provide practical ideas regarding curriculum, staffing, professional development, materials, assessment, and school politics for educators interested in adapting the approaches described here to their own classrooms and school communities.

- Encourage others to adapt and extend the ideas presented here and to join us in an ongoing dialogue about successful practices for developing stronger readers in middle and high school.

Audience

This book will assist middle school and high school classroom teachers in improving their students' ability to read materials ranging from textbooks to Web pages to novels and will increase students' interest in reading on their own. It will offer guidance to middle- and senior-level administrators such as language arts coordinators and curriculum administrators with responsibility for students' academic performance who are working to improve students' reading at the school or district level. The book will help middle and high school principals support teachers' efforts to increase students' reading ability. And finally, the book will inform educational policymakers and academics who are interested in issues of literacy, equity, and achievement.

Overview of the Contents

Part One introduces the concepts underlying our reading apprenticeship approach. We discuss both the need for improved reading ability among middle and high school students and the reasons we are optimistic that these students can learn not only to read textbooks and related materials with increased understanding but also to make reading an important part of their lives beyond the classroom (Chapter One). We then examine the complexity of reading and the importance of *cognitive apprenticeships* in its development. We offer a framework for understanding reading apprenticeship, based in four dimensions of classroom learning, and an overview of instructional approaches that support reading development for adolescent learners (Chapter Two).

Part Two describes how we have put the reading apprenticeship approach into practice. First, we set the scene with an overview of the students and curriculum of Academic Literacy, the yearlong reading course that we all helped conceptualize and design and that two of us taught to ninth graders at Thurgood Marshall Academic High School (Chapter Three). Then we present the ways we have put our theories into action, with detailed descriptions of the specific activities we used in Academic Literacy that have greatly improved not only our students' reading abilities but also the way our students think about reading (Chapters Four, Five, and Six). We then examine the ways our colleagues in the Strategic Literacy Network are embedding a reading apprenticeship approach in their regular English, science, social studies, and math classes (Chapter

Seven). Finally, we discuss some of the challenges we and our colleagues face in implementing a reading apprenticeship approach in the light of diverse student needs, curriculum pressures, and increasing demands for testing and accountability (Chapter Eight).

In Part Three we discuss ideas for professional development and school-wide work toward implementing a reading apprenticeship approach. We describe the methods we have used to help teachers become aware of their own reading skills, acquire a better understanding of the struggles students are experiencing with reading, and prepare to assume the role of master reader to their apprentice reader students (Chapter Nine). We conclude by suggesting ways teachers and administrators might create support for a schoolwide reading apprenticeship program (Chapter Ten).

Our aim in this book is to give readers a new way to think about teaching reading in all subject area classes. We encourage you to experiment with the key ideas, core practices, and sample lessons we weave throughout the book and to adapt and expand on ideas that you find promising. In the Epilogue we tell you how to get in touch with us; we ask you to share with us the impact of these ideas on your classrooms, your teaching, and your students; and we invite you to involve yourself in an ongoing, professional conversation.

Acknowledgments

We thank our many teaching colleagues who contributed to the work described in this book. Mark Salinas and Matthew Clayton were the risk-taking social studies teachers who piloted the Academic Literacy course with their English teacher colleagues at Thurgood Marshall Academic High School. In addition, we are grateful to Dr. Samuel O. Butscher, principal of Thurgood Marshall, for his strong administrative support of Academic Literacy.

We are indebted to the teachers in the Strategic Literacy Network, whose work has expanded the ideas developed in the Academic Literacy classes. In particular, we want to thank those whose classroom work is described and cited in Chapter Seven: Don Berry, Fran Coon, Jordona Elderts, Gina Hale, Rita Jensen, Darleen Kallas, Lisa Morehouse, Nicci Nunes, Caro Pemberton, Stan Pesick, Lynn Slobodien, Tim Tindol, Marcia Weisman, and Peter Williamson. They have given us wonderful examples of ways to embed a reading apprenticeship into regular English, social studies, science, and math classrooms.

Our reader reviewers worked through many stages of this book: Jane Braunger, Carolyn Fairbrook, Pete Feeley, Ellen Hershey, Krista Rogerson, Martha Hoppe, Marean Jordan, Faith Nitschke, Jill Shallenberger, and Peter Thacker. All were generous with their time, encouragement, and thoughtful comments. We thank Jane Braunger additionally for her timely help in later stages of our work on the book.

Many colleagues at WestEd have been important to our work on this book. We are grateful to Glen Harvey, Gary Estes, Don Barfield, and Kate Jamentz for providing institutional support and personal encouragement. Our colleague in the Strategic Literacy Initiative (SLI), Faye Mueller, has made invaluable contributions to the research on which this book is based.

Our other SLI colleagues, Michael Pipkin, Tamara Reeder, and Sherri Young, also helped in the development of this book in many ways. Colleagues Paul Smicker, James Al-Shamma, and Bela Evans in WestEd's technical support department provided important help, as did Tom Ross, WestEd's librarian.

Joy Zimmerman, a member of WestEd's communications staff, provided great assistance with developmental editing and did so with good humor and patience.

Lesley Iura and Christie Hakim, education editor and associate editor at Jossey-Bass, have been gracious in their support and encouragement for our book since we began work on it. We also acknowledge Elspeth MacHattie for her superb copyediting.

There would have been no reading improvement work to describe without the generous support over many years of The Stuart Foundations, the William and Flora Hewlett Foundation, the San Francisco Foundation, the MacArthur/Spencer Professional Development Research and Documentation Program, the Walter S. Johnson Foundation, and the Gabilan Foundation. In addition, support from the U.S. Department of Education's Office of Educational Research and Improvement funded part of our work on an early version of this manuscript. The Rockefeller Foundation, through its Collaborative on Humanities and Arts Teaching program, directed by Judith Renyi, initiated support together with the San Francisco Education Fund for the Humanities Education, Research, and Language Development (HERALD)—the forerunner of the SLI. In addition, we are grateful for the support provided to the HERALD Project by the San Francisco Unified School District (SFUSD). SFUSD's Acting Superintendent Linda Davis (then Deputy Superintendent) was especially helpful, providing insight and ongoing encouragement from 1988 to 1996.

Ellen Hershey, a colleague, program officer, and reviewer of various drafts, has our special thanks for having believed in the potential of the project that developed into our reading apprenticeship approach long before it was clear that it would bear fruit.

We are also grateful to a group of scholar colleagues—Carne Barnett, Sarah Freedman, Peg Griffin, Shirley Brice Heath, Glynda Hull, Carol Lee, Paul LeMahieu, Judith Warren Little, Milbrey McLaughlin, P. David Pearson, Mike Rose, Nadine Rosenthal, Judy Shulman, and Richard Sterling—whose ideas and personal encouragement have informed our work both directly and indirectly over many years. In addition, we are indebted to National Writing Project colleagues across the country—particularly Judy Buchanan,

Elyse Eidman-Aadahl, and Jo Fyfe—whose works form part of the foundation of our own.

We thank the students at Thurgood Marshall Academic High School, students in the many classrooms of our colleagues in the SLI, and the other children in our lives, especially Evan King, Beth Kissack, and Eric Kissack, whose spirit, humor, and persistence inspires our work and continually challenges us to find new answers to difficult questions.

The members of our book group have provided nourishment and camaraderie for our own reading—a welcome counterpoint to our professional reading and writing.

Finally, all of us have been sustained by our family members, colleagues, and friends through the challenges of telling this story. To all of them—David Arehart, Sandra Backovich, Naomi Bunis, Laura Finkler, Peg Griffin, Arlan Hurwitz, Roz Leiser, Elizabeth McGee, Carrie, David, and Hannah Schoenbach, and especially to Lynn Eden, Paul King, and Richard Sterling—our heartfelt thanks.

San Francisco, California
July 1999

Ruth Schoenbach
Cynthia Greenleaf
Christine Cziko
Lori Hurwitz

The Sponsor

WestEd is a nonprofit education research, development, and service agency headquartered in San Francisco, with offices elsewhere in California and in Arizona, Massachusetts, and Washington, D.C. WestEd's researchers and policy analysts conduct wide-ranging programs aimed at improving education and other opportunities for children, youths, and adults.

The Strategic Literacy Initiative (SLI) is a collaborative research, development, and service organization based in San Francisco at WestEd. The SLI works with educators and communities to develop the literacy skills of adolescents; their mission is to expand the academic, creative, career, and civic opportunities of young people through higher-level literacy development.

The SLI develops text and videotaped literacy case studies of adolescent readers, provides inquiry-based professional development for teams of middle and high school teachers, provides teachers with access to relevant research and resources, and studies the impact of its programs on both student and teacher learning.

The initiative is supported through funding from The Stuart Foundations, the William and Flora Hewlett Foundation, the Spencer Foundation, the MacArthur Foundation, the Gabilan Foundation, and the San Francisco Foundation, in addition to contracts with schools, districts, county offices of education, and a variety of school reform networks.

The Authors

Ruth Schoenbach is project director for the Strategic Literacy Initiative (SLI) at WestEd. From 1988 to 1996 she directed the Humanities Education, Research, and Language Development (HERALD) Project in the San Francisco Unified School District, where she had worked previously as a classroom teacher and curriculum developer. She has a master's degree from the Harvard Graduate School of Education.

Cynthia Greenleaf is associate director for the SLI at WestEd, where she leads the initiative's research efforts. For the past fifteen years she has provided professional development and support for secondary teachers and studied the impact of classroom innovations on student learning opportunities and achievement, winning several national awards for her research on classroom-based literacy development. She has a Ph.D. in Language and Literacy from the Graduate School of Education at the University of California at Berkeley.

Christine Cziko is academic coordinator of the Multicultural Urban Secondary Education program at the University of California at Berkeley Graduate School of Education. She taught English for twenty-five years in New York City and San Francisco public schools and worked as a teacher consultant for the New York City Writing Project. She was the lead teacher in creating and implementing Academic Literacy at Thurgood Marshall High School.

Lori Hurwitz is a teacher in the English Department at Thurgood Marshall Academic High School in San Francisco and is currently pursuing a master's degree at the University of California at Berkeley. She teaches Academic Literacy and, as a teacher consultant to the SLI, assists other schools to implement Academic Literacy courses.

Reading for Understanding

Part One

Confronting the Problem of Middle and High School Reading

Chapter 1

Rethinking the Problem: Crisis and Opportunity

My nightmare is that many middle school students aren't reading at grade level, or if they are, they won't read the class assignments anyway. Consequently, I find myself trying to avoid getting students involved in reading by assigning as little reading as possible. I teach around reading in order to make sure students understand science.

A middle school teacher

When I started, high school was a real challenge. All these books were thrown on my desk and I was told to read them. I know it will be even harder when I get to college.

A tenth-grade student

THE HEADLINE-MAKING reading wars of recent years—pitting phonics against whole language in the early reading arena—have obscured the less visible but highly critical issue of reading above elementary grades. Yet among middle and high school teachers across the country, a quiet crisis has been brewing. This quiet crisis focuses on the reading abilities of adolescent students. Teachers' concerns—and increasingly those of administrators and policymakers as well—center on the fact that many of their students have difficulty dealing with *academic texts*, the range of reading materials students are expected to read and comprehend in the middle and high school academic curriculum.

Nevertheless, our recent work with students and teachers in using an approach we call reading apprenticeship demonstrates that teachers can make a considerable difference in these older students' reading abilities. It is not too late for these students to come to think of themselves as able readers, capable of employing books and articles for formal, assigned learning and, perhaps just as important, capable of using written materials of all kinds for learning on their own and for entertainment. In these first two chapters we address some causes of students' reading challenges and discuss the rationale behind our approach and its current success.

The Quiet Crisis

The democratic aim of having a broader spectrum of students attain higher levels of academic achievement than at any previous time in U.S. history drives a good deal of current education reform. The prominence of the national and state standards movement is evidence of this emphasis. Meeting the challenge of higher standards is difficult in all the academic domains. In reading, national tests reveal that although the majority of U.S. students can read at a "basic" level, they cannot read and comprehend the types of higher-level texts essential to an individual's success in an information-based economy.[1] Such tests tell us what most secondary teachers already know: students' limited reading proficiency keeps them from accomplishing the challenging work necessary to meet high academic standards.

Teachers who work with low-achieving students often feel particularly frustrated by poor reading. They may feel especially overwhelmed when contemplating the distance between what they perceive their students' academic achievement to be and the expectations set out in reform documents about what students should know and be able to do in each subject area.

But low academic literacy is by no means an issue only for poorly performing students. Even among those who do relatively well in class and score reasonably well on standardized tests, teachers can point to students who have difficulty comprehending and interpreting class texts, who fail to complete reading assignments, and who seem unlikely to become independent, lifelong readers. "You can't rely on the students to read," explains one middle school teacher we know. "They will engage in projects, but they don't seem to read or understand the source materials or texts."

When faced with students' resistance to reading or difficulty in comprehending course materials, teachers respond in a variety of ways. Feeling pressed to cover the curriculum, unprepared to assist students with reading, and eager to make sure students understand the content of a particular discipline, many find themselves teaching around reading. They make adjustments that may seem sensible but that they know to be compromises. "I'm doing backflips in the classroom to get the content across without expecting them to read the textbook," one history teacher told us. "I've stopped assigning reading; the text is almost supplementary for my history curriculum," admitted another.

Hitting the Literacy Ceiling

We have come to refer to students' difficulty with reading and understanding subject area texts as the *literacy ceiling*—a ceiling that limits what students can hope to achieve both in the classroom and in their lives outside of school. Naturally, the literacy ceiling also limits what a teacher can hope to achieve in his or her classroom. To the degree that students cannot independently access the knowledge and information embedded in the books and other printed materials that are part of a curriculum, teachers must offer alternative ways for them to acquire it.

Many middle and high school teachers with whom we have discussed student reading express frustration, sometimes in terms of blame: "Why didn't somebody do a better job earlier of preparing these students to read what they need to read to succeed at this grade level?" Others express a sense of inadequacy and bewilderment: "What am I supposed to do when they can barely get through a page in the textbook on their own? I'm a subject area teacher, not a reading teacher!" Perhaps the most disconcerting response is the resigned despair inherent in the frequently heard opinion that "it's too late for these students to catch up."

Teachers and policymakers are not the only ones worried about the literacy ceiling. Students faced daily with the difficulty of making sense of the unfamiliar texts and tasks of the secondary curriculum have a much more immediate and personal cause for concern. Many find reading mystifying and have secretly come to believe that they are just not cut out to be readers. Some face reading challenges with a mounting sense of exasperation, knowing how to read the individual words but not how to even begin making sense of sentences, paragraphs, and chapters.

Students also make their own adjustments to reading difficulties, often avoiding a reading task entirely and waiting for a teacher to tell them what they need to know. Students who have come to think of themselves as nonreaders or poor readers develop various survival strategies. Some attempt invisibility, sliding silently down in their seats in hopes that they won't be called on. Others act out, creating distractions when they fear their errors or inadequacies are about to be exposed. Still others adopt a stance that clearly says, "I don't care about school at all." The most dedicated among them—or perhaps simply those with the most stamina—struggle through assigned texts painfully.

Unproductive Responses to the Problem

It's Too Late

Concerns about academic literacy have given rise to a number of well-intentioned but misguided and, we believe, ultimately unproductive responses in the education community. Underlying them all is a pervasive sense among educators that if students have not become effective, independent readers before middle school the window of opportunity has closed.

The idea that at age eleven, fourteen, or seventeen it is too late to become a strong and independent reader of academic texts is both insidious and self-perpetuating. Ironically, this idea is unintentionally reinforced by the recent and justifiable emphasis placed on early reading. The importance of students' becoming competent and engaged readers early in their school careers is inarguable. However, the assumption that children who have not become good readers in the early grades will never catch up is both incorrect and destructive. Further, the companion assumption that children who learn to read well in those early years have no need of further reading instruction is also misguided.

Such assumptions are based on a narrow, incomplete, and unproductive view of learning to read. Mastery of the technical skill of *decoding*—sounding out and pronouncing the words on a page—is only a part of reading development. Successful readers develop over time through a continuous process of learning to make sense of varied and increasingly complex texts. Adolescents have many important intellectual resources they can marshal to become stronger readers. However, by working with them primarily at a word skill level, well-meaning educators cut off these important sources of strength for developing higher-level reading abilities.

Indeed, the belief that reading is essentially a process of saying the words rather than actively constructing meaning from texts is widespread among many students. For instance, one of the students we interviewed looked surprised when he was asked to describe the topic discussed in a section of text he had just read. "I don't know what it was about," he answered, with no sense of irony. "I was busy reading. I wasn't paying attention."

Back to the Beginning

One of the key goals in teaching is to support students' development as active, engaged, and independent learners. Yet a common response to low academic literacy actually moves students in the opposite direction, taking struggling readers back to the beginning of the learning-to-read process by reteaching them to decode words. This response is based on a belief that students' reading difficulties are rooted in an inability to sound out words rather than in a lack of explicit instruction in reading comprehension strategies and a lack of extensive opportunities to read.

The idea that early reading instruction has failed to equip middle and high school students with adequate decoding skills is pervasive. It has been spread in part by groups of parents, researchers, and policymakers who have raised public alarm about what they see as insufficient phonics instruction. Yet most adolescents whom teachers might initially describe as "not able to even get the words off the page" are far less likely to have problems with decoding than with comprehension, unfamiliar vocabulary, insufficient background knowledge, reading fluency, or engagement.[2] Typically, these students have neither been expected to do much reading nor assisted with reading in school. As a result they have very little stamina or persistence when they encounter difficulties with texts.

In our own work with middle and high school students, we find decoding problems quite rare. In fact, after one team of middle school teachers with whom we have worked became convinced that the students identified as the lowest-skilled readers in the school were unable to decode, the team asked a reading specialist to test them. But the specialist found that even though comprehension problems were widespread among these culturally and linguistically diverse children of the working poor, decoding problems were almost nonexistent.

For such students, being sent back to the beginning of reading instruction only reinforces their misconception that reading is just saying the words. This response does nothing to help students understand or use the complex comprehension processes and the knowledge about texts and the world that good readers rely on. Moreover, by simply reteaching decoding, educators ignore one of the most powerful resources for reading improvement: the knowledge and cognitive resources that adolescents already use constantly in their lives beyond the school walls.

Searching for a Skills-in-a-Box Solution

In our work with secondary schools over the past several years, we have been asked repeatedly for "programs" that provide "proven results" for student reading achievement. It is easy to understand why this question comes up as often as it does. Unfortunately, there is simply no quick fix for reading difficulties. Over two decades of research has shown that reading is a complex cognitive and social practice. In building reading aptitude, there is no skills-only approach that can substitute for extensive reading. On the contrary, repeated studies have demonstrated that instruction in isolated grammar, decoding, or comprehension skills may have little or no impact on students' activity while actually reading.[3]

When used by knowledgeable and skillful teachers, some commercial programs and products can support students' motivation, engagement, and sense of agency. Teachers can also use these programs to help students become more focused on integrating an expanded repertoire of skills and strategies into their reading. But we believe schools' limited resources would be better spent on enriching classroom and school libraries and on building the knowledge and teaching repertoires of subject area teachers rather than on purchasing packaged reading programs that remain separate from the reading that takes place in subject area classrooms.

Talking the Text

Many middle school teachers and most high school teachers see their primary responsibility as teaching the important ideas and knowledge base of their disciplines—the *content*. Filling in orally what students are either not able or not willing to learn from the course texts is a natural response for any dedicated teacher. Making a strategic decision to provide the entire class with alternative means of accessing the ideas and content of the curriculum, teachers may read to students, *talk through* the book, or show a related video. As one history teacher explained, "Because you can't rely on students to read, I feel like I'm constantly summarizing the history textbook so kids don't miss the main points. I wish I didn't have to assume that role as much, but I find I do."[4]

Many students now seem to regard such compensatory practices as normal because they are so common. One student offered us this description of how reading is handled in her science class, and it could easily apply to any number of classrooms we have observed: "Usually, the teacher just writes stuff on the overhead. Then we copy it down and she gives us lots of labs to do. I don't remember using the book. We probably only used it a couple of times to look for stuff."

The strategy of teaching content without having students read or by asking them to read only small amounts becomes a self-perpetuating instructional practice. When students are unprepared to approach reading assignments independently, many teachers give up any thought of holding them accountable for reading. Then, because these students do not have to read in some subject area classes, they resist expectations that they will do so in other classes. Finally the teachers of the other classes begin to give up their expectations that students will read academic texts independently. In this way, concerned and caring teachers inadvertently enable students to continue up the grades with very limited reading abilities. This reinforces students' dependence on teachers rather than their own independent reading to access and interpret information and curriculum content.

To perpetuate such dependence on teachers is to deny students opportunities they can gain only through the extensive, independent reading of texts. Students may find many texts they are asked to read difficult or boring, unrelated to their lives, and unfamiliar both in language and conceptual content. Yet if students are to have an expanded range of future options, they must have the confidence and the will to approach such texts and the ability to make sense of them when they choose to do so.

However, without being encouraged and supported to expand the limits of their reading, many students may never be prepared to independently read *gatekeeper texts*. These are the various texts that permit or deny students access to educational, economic, civic, and cultural opportunities. Examples include the SAT test excerpts that assess understanding; reading tests for entry-level jobs; college and job applications; textbooks and other reading material for postsecondary education and training; and even directions for applying for a student loan or home mortgage.

Protecting Them from Boredom

Anyone who has read a range of secondary school textbooks knows that many are neither well written nor engaging. That is one reason we strongly support the efforts of so many teachers and other educators to create carefully designed curricula that incorporate a variety of genres of writing as well as primary source documents.

At the same time, we know that boring, poorly written, and seemingly irrelevant texts are a fact of life—not only in school but on the job and even at home (consider tax preparation manuals, for instance). If students are to succeed in school and beyond, they must be willing and able to work their way through and make sense of even some poorly written texts.

Many educators tell us that students shouldn't have to read texts that are written in a dry or abstract style or that employ an unfamiliar narrative sequence or style. They argue that students shouldn't have to read texts that students find boring, irrelevant, or inaccessible. Why require students to read *The Time Machine*? Why assign Shakespeare? Why have students read the history textbook? Unfortunately, as we have learned from years of experience with many teachers who have created engaging curricula using primary source documents and other relevant texts, students often have as much difficulty with these texts as they have with less engaging texts. The problem clearly goes well beyond the materials provided for students to read.

Of course schools should provide students with well-written, interesting, and varied texts in the various academic disciplines so that students will be more able and likely to actually read and understand them. And of course teaching students to read books of their own choosing is vitally important for building their motivation, fluency, and engagement as readers. But taken to its extreme, an emphasis on engagement and relevance alone can turn into never asking students to read or learn anything they are not already interested in. Additionally, if teachers take the position that they should "protect" students from texts that are or are perceived to be difficult, poorly written, boring, biased, or irrelevant, they may contribute, however unwittingly, to keeping low-performing students at the tail end of the educational opportunity curve. This tactic may contribute to a widening gulf of unequal access to opportunities in today's increasingly knowledge-based society.

Through our work we have come to believe that teachers must help students learn and internalize strategies for persisting with and understanding texts that students perceive as boring or irrelevant. We have a responsibility to help adolescent readers learn to approach these texts as informed, critical thinkers. Armed with appropriate strategies and mental habits, they can then make their own decisions about which texts they will or won't work through—decisions based on their *goals* and not on their reading ability.

Our experience also tells us that once students are given methods for comprehending difficult and seemingly boring texts, they often find these texts more interesting. Students do like to learn; they do want to become competent and knowledgeable. As we heard one particularly articulate young woman tell a roomful of high school teachers, "We know we aren't very well educated. We know there are things we should know by now that we don't. But we're not stupid; most of us are really smart. You just need to show us, break it down for us, work with us and expect us to do it."

The Case for Optimism

In spite of all the problems and challenges, we see a strong case for optimism about the possibility of significantly improving students' reading in secondary schools. Our optimism is rooted in our experiences with students and teachers who have been involved in the kinds of learning we describe throughout this book.

We are convinced that all students can and should receive instruction that enables them to make sense of many types of texts. Working in collaboration with a variety of middle and high school teachers and their students over the past several years, we have begun to develop what we believe is a highly effective approach for providing such instruction.[5] It enables a range of teachers—from first-year science teachers to twenty-year veteran history teachers—to incorporate reading instruction within their subject area classes without adding new curriculum.

Context for Optimism:
A Teacher Researcher Community

Two of us are high school teachers from the San Francisco Bay Area, and two of us are senior staff members of a literacy research and professional development project at WestEd—a nonprofit education research, development, and service agency headquartered in the Bay Area.[6] We began working together in 1995 when WestEd's Strategic Literacy Initiative (SLI) staff enlisted teacher teams from three Bay Area high schools to participate in a combination professional development and research effort focusing on student literacy. The specific intent was to conduct collaborative, action-oriented research aimed at identifying what secondary school subject area teachers could do to help their students become better readers of academic and other challenging texts. This teacher-researcher collaboration came together as the Strategic Literacy Network (SLN), which subsequently expanded to include teacher teams from middle schools as well.

The network's collaborative research took two forms: first, we studied and adapted the findings from existing research on reading comprehension, little of which had focused on middle or high school students, and second, we undertook new research on the network teachers' struggling adolescent readers. Specifically, we developed detailed video- and text-based case studies of a group of thirty ninth-grade students identified by their teachers as representative of the range of students who had difficulty reading and understanding assigned texts. The objective was to discover the ways adolescent readers were presently carrying out classroom reading assignments and to develop, adapt, and pilot teaching practices that seemed to have potential for improving students' ability to more independently make sense of discipline-specific texts.

Over a two-year period, SLI researchers and participating network teachers gathered a wealth of information about student reading practices, patterns, and attitudes. We carried out in-depth *reading history* interviews with students, videotaped students reading and discussing texts, and developed the case studies described previously. This information gave us a number of windows into student reading performance. To this rich mix we added documentation of teachers' reflections on and analysis of student performance.

Against this background, network researchers and teachers also pored over the existing research on reading comprehension, identifying information that might aid the teachers in better helping their students. Out of all this research and study emerged, over time, an approach to improving secondary students' reading in general and their reading of academic texts in particular through the implementation of what we call *reading apprenticeship,* a method in which the classroom teacher serves as *master reader* to his or her *student apprentices.*

The network's intent all along had been to identify how subject area teachers could improve student reading in the process of teaching content. But after the first year of work together, teachers from Thurgood Marshall Academic High School were fast concluding that their students needed a more intense intervention than could be provided by embedding reading apprenticeship approaches in regular subject area classes. What was needed, they believed, was a stand-alone course focused solely and explicitly on academic reading and thus was born Marshall's yearlong course titled Academic Literacy. Other network teachers meanwhile continued to work to embed a reading apprenticeship approach in their subject area courses. For these reasons, the reading apprenticeship approach has developed in two contexts: standing alone in a required course for incoming freshmen at an urban high school and embedded in discipline-specific classes at other Bay Area middle and high schools.

At the heart of the reading apprenticeship approach to reading instruction is the network members' strong conviction that teachers and their students possess a powerful set of untapped resources for improving student reading. That conviction has been born out by assessment evidence from both the stand-alone course and the subject area courses. The results show the reading apprenticeship approach yielding great progress not only in student reading achievement but also in students' growing sense of themselves as lifelong independent readers.

Teachers' Untapped Resources

"I realized that thinking about what I did when I read had strong parallels to the writing process approach that I had been using in my classes for years. It was like a light had been turned on. I did know what a competent reader had to do in order to make sense of text—I was doing it all the time. Now the challenge was to make the strategies I used explicit first to myself and then to my students."[7] As this teacher discovered, people whose education has prepared them to teach English, history, science, or math have a great deal of knowledge about how to make sense of and use information from the various texts typical of their disciplines. This knowledge has helped them be successful in their own education. They continue to draw on this knowledge as they read in their fields and prepare lessons in their disciplines. Most, however, have not spent much time thinking about the mental processes by which they make sense of these texts, and few middle and high school teachers see their own abilities to read subject area texts as a powerful resource for helping students approach these texts independently, confidently, and successfully.

The reading apprenticeship approach to improving student reading taps into this knowledge. More specifically, it relies on teachers working with other teachers to make conscious their own reading processes—the hitherto unrecognized knowledge and strategies that good readers rely on to read effectively. As teachers become more aware of the complex ways they themselves make sense of text, they gain new appreciation for the reading difficulties students may face. They can then begin to apprentice their students to the reading craft by making their own normally invisible comprehension processes visible to those students. As apprentices, students in turn become empowered as readers, able to tap and expand their own knowledge. In the course of doing so, they begin to *own* and improve their reading process.

Students' Untapped Resources

In the classroom we tend to view students through the narrow lens of academic competency. A teacher frustrated by students' inability or unwillingness to read academic texts can come to define students primarily through their literacy problems. But the life experience of adolescents, particularly as manifested in their strategic behaviors and nimbleness with language, offers a wealth of resources that can give them strategic control over reading comprehension. We have come to see secondary school students as young adults with powerful resources that can be tapped in a learning environment that is safe, respectful, and collaborative. As teachers work with—rather than against—some of the common developmental characteristics of adolescents, teachers and students can begin to build a reading inquiry partnership, or master reader–apprentice relationship.

The social goals of adolescents can serve the academic goals of teachers when the learning environment is carefully constructed to promote social collaboration. Adolescents are at the point of trying on and forming new identities. Precisely at this time in their lives, they can be encouraged to try on new reader identities, to realize that a lot of who they will become and what they will do in their lives is in their own hands.

Many adolescents also recognize and try to conceal their own academic deficits. They are thus exquisitely sensitive to situations that might result in humiliation in front of their peers. However, in a learning environment in which the skill of being able to point to specific confusions with texts is expected and valued, young people's sensitivities to their reading difficulties can become an invaluable asset.

The natural desire of many adolescents to participate in creating something larger than themselves can also be a motivating factor supporting their work on improving reading.[8] A thin veneer of cynicism notwithstanding, most young people want to serve, to make a difference, to make the world a better place. This desire to change the world, added to their self-interest in future educational and job opportunities, can motivate adolescents to master what Lisa Delpit has called *power codes* of our society, including the standards and conventions of written language.[9]

Mining Students' and Teachers' Resources

In a reading apprenticeship, teachers invite students to become partners in a collaborative inquiry into their reading processes. The aim is to help students become better readers by making the teacher's reading processes visible to them, by helping them gain insight into their own reading processes, and by having them learn a repertoire of cognitive problem-solving strategies. As the students gain practice in becoming aware of and controlling their own reading processes, they yield additional information for their teacher about the social contexts, strategies, knowledge bases, and understandings they bring to the task of making sense of texts. A reading apprenticeship is at heart a partnership of expertise, drawing both on what subject area teachers know and do as disciplinary readers and on adolescents' unique and often underestimated strengths as learners.

Signs of Success

In October 1996, four teachers working with the Strategic Literacy Initiative began teaching a new course—Academic Literacy—to incoming ninth graders at Thurgood Marshall Academic High School in San Francisco. By May of that same school year, the approximately two hundred students pre- and post-tested had improved their reading comprehension from an average late seventh-grade level to an average late ninth-grade level, as measured on a norm-referenced reading test (see Chapter Ten).[10] That gain is roughly equivalent to moving from being able to independently read books at the level of *Charlotte's Web* to independently reading books at the level of *To Kill a Mockingbird*.

These gains in test scores were consistent across all ethnic groups and across four different classrooms in which four different teachers implemented a course based on reading apprenticeship. The test score gains were accompanied by impressive and equally important changes in student reading attitudes and habits. As one ninth grader told us, "What I can really do what I didn't do before was think about what the book is saying and try to reflect and give some thought to what is going on in the book instead of closing it and not thinking anything when I read it." In addition to becoming more interested in reading for pleasure, students gained knowledge and confidence as strategic readers of a variety of texts.

A year later, follow-up studies on students for whom we were able to get test data showed not only that these reading gains were holding but that these students had continued to grow at an accelerated rate, as measured by the standardized reading test. In interviews, tenth-grade students told us how they were using what they learned in Academic Literacy for school, in testing situations, and in their daily lives. This combination of positive quantitative and qualitative outcomes provides reason for hope that the quiet crisis of reading in secondary school content classes is not the intractable problem it has sometimes seemed to be. And there is still more good news. Test and survey data from the classrooms of teachers who are embedding a reading apprenticeship approach in their subject area courses suggest yet more reason for optimism.[11]

As a group, the students of Strategic Literacy teachers made statistically significant gains on a norm-referenced test of reading comprehension, making greater than average growth in reading. These students gained ground in comparison to the testmakers' norming sample of grade-matched peers, significantly narrowing the achievement gap for these diverse, urban students. In addition, SLN students' beliefs about themselves as readers, their reading habits and attitudes, and their knowledge of strategies for approaching reading tasks showed growth similar to that of students in Academic Literacy.

Notes

Epigraph: W. P. Bintz, "Exploring Reading Nightmares of Middle and Secondary School Teachers," *Journal of Adolescent and Adult Literacy,* 1997, *41*(1), 12–24.

1. P. L. Donahue, K. E. Voelkl, J. R. Campbell, and J. Mazzeo, *The NAEP 1998 Reading Report Card for the Nation and the States* (Washington, D.C.: National Center for Education Statistics, 1999).

2. D. E. Alverman and D. W. Moore. "Secondary School Reading," in R. Barr, M. L. Kamil, P. Mosenthal, and P. D. Pearson (eds.), *Handbook of Reading*

Research, Vol. 2. (New York: Longman, 1991, pp. 951–983); R. Calfee and P. Drum. "Research on Teaching Reading," in M. C. Wittrock (ed.), *Handbook of Research on Teaching,* 3rd ed. (New York: Macmillan, 1986, pp. 804–849); J. T. Guthne and D. E. Alverman (eds.), *Engaged Reading: Processes, Practices, and Policy Implications* (New York: Teachers College Press, 1991).

3. L. G. Fielding and D. P. Pearson, "Reading Comprehension: What Works," *Educational Leadership,* Feb. 1994, pp. 62–68.

4. Quoted in C. Greenleaf and others, "Close Readings: Developing Inquiry Tools and Processes for Generative Professional Development," paper presented at the annual meeting of the American Educational Research Association, Montreal, Apr. 1999.

5. Greenleaf and others, "Close Readings."

6. For further information about WestEd, the Strategic Literacy Initiative, and available resources please visit the WestEd Web site [www.wested.org].

7. Quoted in C. Cziko, "Reading Happens in Your Mind, Not in Your Mouth: Teaching and Learning 'Academic Literacy' in an Urban High School," *California English,* Summer 1998, 3(4), p. 6.

8. J. Davidson and D. Koppenhaver, *Adolescent Literacy: What Works and Why,* 2nd ed. (New York: Garland, 1993).

9. L. D. Delpit, *Other People's Children: Cultural Conflict in the Classroom* (New York: New Press, 1995).

10. C. Greenleaf and others, "Apprenticing Adolescent Readers to Academic Literacy." Paper presented at the annual meeting of the American Educational Research Association, Montreal, Apr. 1999.

11. Greenleaf and others, "Close Readings."

Chapter 2

The Reading Apprenticeship Framework

IT IS PROBABLY self-evident that the conceptions educators hold about the nature of reading shape their approaches to helping students improve their reading abilities. As we noted in Chapter One, some current approaches to supporting adolescent reading improvement address students' word-level reading problems as a precondition for working on other levels of reading improvement. Our reading apprenticeship approach is different because our understanding of the nature of reading is different. Here is a brief outline of what we have learned from existing research and our own observation.

What Is Reading?

Reading is not just a basic skill. Many people think of reading as a skill that is taught once and for all in the first few years of school. In this view of reading the credit (or blame) for students' reading ability goes to primary grade teachers, and upper elementary and secondary school teachers at each grade level need teach only new vocabulary and concepts relevant to new content. Seen this way, reading is a simple process: readers decode (figure out how to pronounce) each word in a text and then automatically comprehend the meaning of the words, as they do with their everyday spoken language. This is not our understanding of reading.

Reading is a complex process. Think for a moment about the last thing you read. A student essay? A school bulletin? A newspaper analysis of rising conflict in another part of the world? A report on water quality in your community? A novel? If you could recapture your mental processing, you would notice that you read with reference to a particular *world* of knowledge and experience related to the text. The text evoked voices, memories, knowledge, and experiences from other times and places—some long dormant, some more immediate. If you were reading complex text about complex ideas or an unfamiliar type of text, you were working to understand it, your reading most likely characterized by many false starts and much backtracking. You were probably trying to relate it to your existing knowledge and understanding. You might have stumbled over unfamiliar words and found yourself trying to interpret them from the context. And you might have found yourself having an internal conversation with the author, silently agreeing or disagreeing with what you read.

As experienced readers read, they begin to generate a mental representation, or *gist*, of the text, which serves as an evolving framework for understanding subsequent parts of the text. As they read further, they test this evolving meaning and monitor their understanding, paying attention to inconsistencies that arise as they interact with the text. If they notice they are losing the meaning as they read, they draw on a variety of strategies to readjust their understandings. They come to texts with purposes that guide their reading, taking a stance toward the text and responding to the ideas that take shape in the conversation between the text and the self.[1]

While reading a newspaper analysis of global hostilities, for example, you may silently argue with its presentation of "facts," question the assertions of the writer, and find yourself revisiting heated debates with friends over U.S. foreign policy. You may picture events televised during earlier wars. Lost in your recollections, you may find that even though your eyes have scanned several paragraphs, you have taken nothing in, so you reread these passages, this time focusing on analysis.

Reading is problem solving. Reading is not a straightforward process of lifting the words off the page. It is a complex process of problem solving in which the reader works to make sense of a text not just from the words and sentences on the page but also from the ideas, memories, and knowledge evoked by those words and sentences. Although at first glance reading may seem to be passive, solitary, and simple, it is in truth active, populated by a rich mix of voices and views—those of the author, of the reader, and of others the reader has heard, read about, and otherwise encountered throughout life.

Fluent reading is not the same as decoding. Skillful reading does require readers to carry out certain tasks in a fairly automatic manner. Decoding skills—quick word recognition and ready knowledge of relevant vocabulary, for example—are essential to successful reading. However, they are by no means sufficient, especially when texts are complex or otherwise challenging.

Yet many discussions about struggling readers confuse decoding with fluency. Fluency derives from the reader's ability not just to decode or identify individual words but also to quickly process larger language units. In our inquiries into reading—our own and that of our students— we have seen that fluency, like other dimensions of reading, varies according to the text at hand. When readers are unfamiliar with the particular language structures and features of a text, their language-processing ability breaks down. This means, for example, that teachers cannot assume that students who fluently read narrative or literary texts will be equally fluent with expository texts or primary source documents.

Fluency begins to develop when students have frequent opportunities to read texts that are easy for them. Multiple rereadings of more difficult texts help broaden a reader's fluency.[2] Perhaps most important for adolescent readers, fluency grows as they have opportunities, support, and encouragement to read a wide range of text types about a wide range of topics.

Reading is situationally bounded. A person who understands one type of text is not necessarily proficient at reading all types. An experienced reader of dessert cookbooks can understand what is meant by "turn out on a wire rack to finish cooling" but may be completely unable to make sense of a legal brief. A political science undergraduate can understand that the phrase "on the other hand I will argue" leads into the author's main point and that the main point will be in contrast to the earlier discussion. But that same undergraduate may feel lost when trying to read the poetry recommended by a friend. A good reader of a motorcycle repair manual can make sense of directions that might stump an English literature professor, but may be unable to comprehend her son's chemistry text. And a chemistry teacher may feel completely insecure when trying to understand some of the original source history materials on a colleague's course reading list.

In other words, reading is influenced by situational factors, among them the experiences readers have had with particular kinds of texts and reading for particular purposes. And just as so-called good or proficient readers do not necessarily read all texts with equal ease or success, a so-called poor or struggling reader will not necessarily have a hard time with all texts. That said, researchers do know some things about those readers who are more consistently effective across a broad range of texts and text types.

Proficient readers share some key characteristics. Different reading researchers emphasize different characteristics of good or proficient reader. However, despite contention in many other areas of reading research, when it comes to proficient readers, widespread agreement has emerged in the form of a set of key habits of proficient readers. This consensus could be summarized as follows:[3]

Good readers are . . .

Mentally engaged,

Motivated to read and to learn,

Socially active around reading tasks,

Strategic in monitoring the interactive processes that assist comprehension:

> *Setting goals that shape their reading processes,*
>
> *Monitoring their emerging understanding of a text, and*
>
> *Coordinating a variety of comprehension strategies to control the reading process.*

Social Support for Learning

Our apprenticeship approach to teaching reading in subject area classes is grounded in our view of learning as a social-cognitive interactive process. In this view, which is based in the work of Russian psychologist L. S. Vygotsky, children's cognitive development is seen as "socially mediated"—that is to say, children learn by participating in activities with "more competent others" who provide support for the parts of the task that children cannot yet do by themselves.[4] These more competent others—parents, siblings, and teachers, for example—gauge their support of the child's participation, encouraging the learner to take on more of the task over time. In doing this—often unconsciously or spontaneously—these guides help children carry out valued activities (talking, cooking, playing ball, reading) more independently over time.

The learning environment created by these more knowledgeable others in collaboration with learners during activities like reading or puzzle solving both supports learners and challenges them to grow. Learners begin to internalize and appropriate (make their own) the varied dimensions of the activity: for instance, its goals and functions, the actions necessary to carry it out, and the kinds of cultural tools necessary or fitting to the task. Through this social learning process, learners' cognitive structures—the ways in which learners think—are shaped.

Cognitive Apprenticeships

This view of socially mediated learning applies not only to activities with observable components such as tying shoes or skating or cooking. It applies equally, and importantly, to activities that are largely cognitive, taking place inside the mind and hidden from view. Researchers working within a social-cognitive tradition have described a variety of *cognitive apprenticeships,* in which the mental activities characteristic of certain kinds of cognitive tasks such as computation, written composition, interpreting texts, and the like are internalized and appropriated by learners through social supports of various kinds.[5] Learning to read is yet another task that requires a cognitive apprenticeship.

Reading Apprenticeships

One literacy educator describes the idea of the cognitive apprenticeship in reading by comparing the process of learning to read with learning to ride a bike. In both cases a more proficient other is present to support the beginner, engaging the beginner in the activity and calling attention to often overlooked or hidden strategies.[6] From the beginning, reading apprentices must be engaged in the whole process of problem solving to make sense of written texts, even if they are initially unable to carry out on their own all the individual strategies and subtasks that go into successful reading. The hidden, cognitive dimensions in particular must be drawn out and made visible to the learner.[7] For adolescents, being shown what goes on behind the curtain of expert reading is especially powerful in helping them gain adult mastery.

Demystifying Reading: Making the Invisible Visible

If students are to employ increasingly sophisticated ways of thinking and of solving a variety of cognitive problems, they need more knowledgeable others from whom they can learn how to carry out these complex activities. Much of what happens with texts in classrooms gives students the mistaken impression that reading comprehension happens by magic. To begin to build a repertoire of activities for reading comprehension, students need to have the reading process demystified. They need to see what happens inside the mind of a proficient reader, someone who is willing to make the invisible visible by externalizing his or her mental activity.

Developing Independent, Strategic Readers

In short, our approach to teaching reading in content area classrooms is based on the idea that the complex habits and activities of skillful readers can be taught. But we do not believe they can be taught by a *transmission* approach to teaching, in which students are shown strategies, asked to practice them, and then expected to be able to use them on their own. Instead we see the kind of teaching and learning environment that can develop students' confidence and competence as readers of various kinds of challenging texts as one that requires the interaction of students and teachers in multiple dimensions of classroom life. It is the orchestration of this interactive teaching and learning environment in classrooms that we call a *reading apprenticeship* approach to developing strategic readers.

In the rest of this chapter we briefly present the multiple dimensions of classroom teaching and learning that make up the reading apprenticeship approach, giving an overview of students' learning opportunities in reading apprenticeship classrooms.

Dimensions of Classroom Life Supporting Reading Apprenticeships

We have developed the following model to describe what we believe are the four key dimensions of classroom life that are necessary to support adolescent reading development (Figure 2.1):

- *Social dimension:* community building in the classroom, including recognizing the resources brought by each member and developing a safe environment for students to be open about their reading difficulties

- *Personal dimension:* developing students' identities and self-awareness as readers, as well as their purposes for reading and goals for reading improvement

- *Cognitive dimension:* developing readers' mental processes, including their problem-solving strategies

- *Knowledge-building dimension:* identifying and expanding the kinds of knowledge readers bring to a text and further develop through interaction with that text

Metacognitive Conversation at the Center

At the center of these interacting dimensions, and tying them together, is an ongoing conversation in which teacher and students think about and discuss their personal relationships to reading, the social environment and resources of the classroom, their cognitive activity, and the kinds of knowledge required to make sense of text. This *metacognitive* conversation is carried on both internally, as teacher and students individually read and consider their own mental processes, and externally, as they talk about

FIGURE 2.1

Dimensions of Classroom Life Supporting Reading Apprenticeship

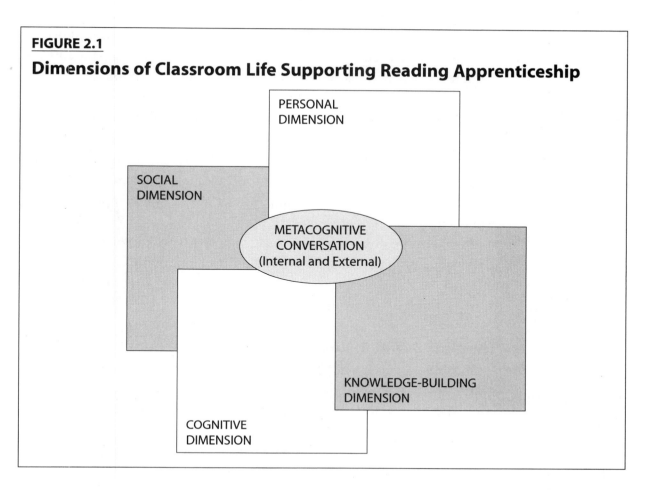

their reading processes, strategies, knowledge resources, and motivations and their interactions with and affective responses to texts.

Metacognition, simply put, is thinking about thinking. As one researcher defines it, "Metacognition refers to one's knowledge concerning one's own cognitive process and products or anything related to them."[8] In metacognitive conversation, then, participants become consciously aware of their mental activity and are able to describe it and discuss it with others. Such conversation enables teachers to make their invisible cognitive activity visible and enables teachers and students to reflectively analyze and assess the impact of their thinking processes. A great deal of research in the past two decades has identified metacognition as key to deep learning and flexible use of knowledge and skills.[9]

The four dimensions of classroom life that support reading apprenticeship are linked by the key enterprise of talking together about making sense of texts. Through metacognition, apprentice readers begin to become aware of their reading processes and, indeed, that there are reading processes. Through many means—class discussions between teachers and students, small-group conversations, written private reflections and logs, personal letters to the teacher or even to characters in books—students can begin to know—and use and further develop—their own minds.

Such conversations and reflections, if they become routine, offer students ongoing opportunities to consider what they are doing as they read—how they are trying to make sense of texts and how well their strategies are working for them. Internal and external conversations about reading processes and the relationships they make possible between and among teachers and students are key to the reading apprenticeship approach.

Furthermore, the social, personal, cognitive, and knowledge-building dimensions of classroom life are linked by metacognitive conversation, and each of these dimensions has its own metacognitive component, as described in the following sections.

The Social Dimension

Establishing a reading apprenticeship classroom begins with the work of nurturing a social environment in which students can begin to reveal their understandings and their struggles as well as to see other students, and their teacher, as potential resources for learning (Figure 2.2). To begin developing this social dimension, teachers work with students to create a sense that they are part of a safe community of readers.

Developing this sense of safety is fundamental to the activity of investigating reading. To help students become more active and strategic readers, we need to hear from the students themselves about what is going on in their minds while they are reading. Therefore they must feel comfortable expressing points of confusion, disagreement, and even disengagement with texts. They need to feel safe enough to talk about where they got lost in a text, what was confusing, what they ordinarily do when they have these kinds of comprehension problems, and how well these strategies work for them.

Motivation to read and to work on improving reading is intimately related to students' cultural and peer group identity. The degree to which students see doing well academically as a means of gaining status with their peers varies.[10] For some students, a stigma may be attached to reading better than others in their social group. Other students may be embarrassed by reading comprehension difficulties, believing these difficulties mean they are not as skilled at reading as they should be. Making it safe for students to discuss reading difficulties mitigates their potential embarrassment. However, for those students who embrace peer cultures that define reading

FIGURE 2.2

Supporting Reading Apprenticeship—The Social Dimension

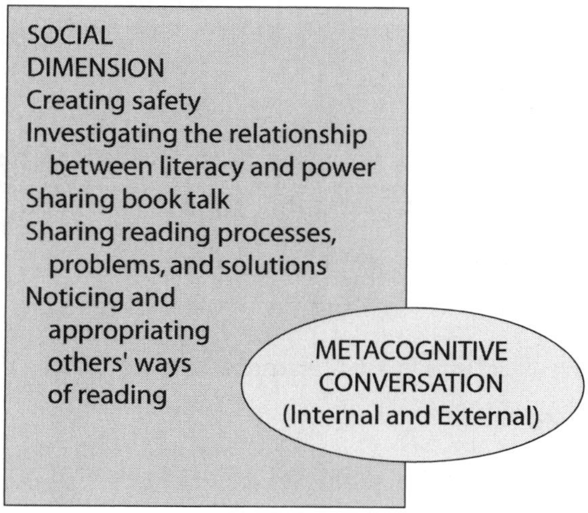

SOCIAL
DIMENSION
Creating safety
Investigating the relationship
   between literacy and power
Sharing book talk
Sharing reading processes,
   problems, and solutions
Noticing and
   appropriating
   others' ways
   of reading

METACOGNITIVE
CONVERSATION
(Internal and External)

negatively, generating interest in reading is critical. Sharing books on topics that appeal to young people is one way of building interest. Another, equally important way is to engage students in asking questions about reading and literacy and its relationship to political, economic, and cultural power.

Here are three kinds of activities that help teachers establish the social dimension of a reading apprenticeship classroom.

Creating Safety
- Talk about what makes it safe or unsafe for students to ask questions or show their confusion in class.
- Agree on classroom rules for discussion so that all students can share their ideas and confusions without being made to feel stupid.
- Talk about what makes it safe or unsafe for students to engage in classroom learning.
- Agree on classroom norms that allow all students to engage in learning activities without being made to feel uncool.

Investigating the Relationship Between Literacy and Power
- Investigate and talk about the people who read in our society, what they read, why they read, and how reading affects their lives.
- Investigate and talk about the people who do not read in our society and how not reading affects their lives

- Read and talk about the historical disenfranchisement through lack of literacy of particular groups of people in this society.

- Talk about the relationships between literacy and power of various kinds, including economic, political, and cultural power.

Sharing Book Talk

- Share the books teachers and classmates have found exciting, fun, interesting, or important.

- Share the ways teachers and classmates choose books they will enjoy and be able to finish for recreational reading.

- Share teachers' and classmates' responses to the ideas, events, and language of texts.

Teachers and students must build a sense of collaborative and respectful inquiry into each other's reading processes. This is key to establishing the conditions for successful reading apprenticeships. Once students are safe to engage in classroom reading activities and share their reading processes and difficulties, the classroom community of readers can offer its members crucial resources in the diversity and breadth of interpretations, experiences, and perspectives that different readers bring to different texts.

Students possess a variety of strengths, including diverse background knowledge and experiences. Each can have times when he or she becomes the more knowledgeable other, helping other students gain comprehension of particular texts and acquire strategies and knowledge for the comprehension of many texts. Teachers act as expert resources for reading strategies, relevant background knowledge, and experience with particular kinds of texts and how they work. In a classroom environment where sharing one's reading processes, comprehension difficulties, and attempts to solve comprehension problems is the norm, teachers have many opportunities to share their expertise. They also can draw students' attention to the fact that different readers in the classroom bring different valuable resources that influence their interpretations of texts.

Two categories of activities in particular develop the social dimension of a reading apprenticeship classroom in which students have access to a variety of resources for dealing with reading comprehension problems.

Sharing Reading Processes, Problems, and Solutions

- Talk about what is confusing in texts.

- Share how teachers and students deal with comprehension problems as they come up in class texts.

- Participate in whole- or small-group problem-solving discussions to make sense of difficult texts.

Noticing and Appropriating Others' Ways of Reading

- Notice the different kinds of background knowledge and experience different readers (teachers and classmates) bring to texts and how that affects the way they interpret what they read.

- Notice the ways different readers *think aloud* and respond to texts as they work to make sense of them.

- Notice the different reading strategies different readers use to make sense of texts.

- Try out the different strategies and approaches other readers use to make sense of texts.

The Personal Dimension

The personal dimension of a reading apprenticeship classroom focuses on developing individual students' relationships to reading in a variety of ways (Figure 2.3). Classroom activities support individual students in developing increased awareness of themselves as readers, inviting them to discover and refine their own goals and motivations, likes and dislikes, and hopes and potential growth in relationship to reading. This work develops within and in turn adds to the development of the social context of the classroom. As individual students gain a sense of themselves as readers, they

---

FIGURE 2.3

Supporting Reading Apprenticeship—The Personal Dimension

PERSONAL
DIMENSION
Developing reader identity
Developing metacognition
Developing reader fluency
   and stamina
Developing reader
   confidence and range

METACOGNITIVE
CONVERSATION
(Internal and External)

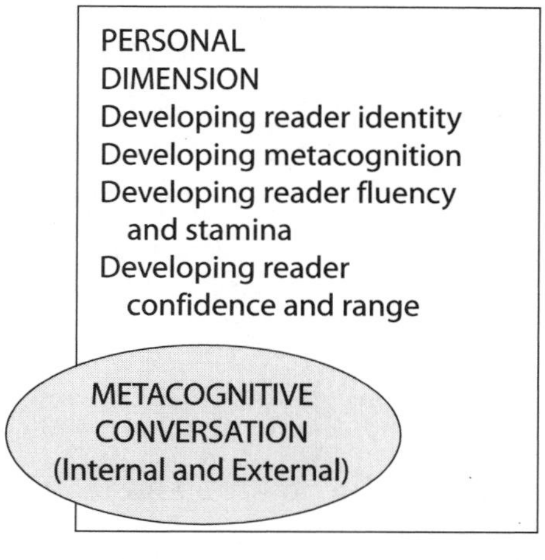

add to the classroom community their descriptions of their varied reading processes, their responses to texts, and their questions and interpretations, all of which provide rich content for classroom discussions.

The activity of reading, the ability to use a variety of metacognitive and cognitive strategies to make sense of texts, is closely tied to the *will* to read.[11] When students feel they are not good readers, frustration, embarrassment, or fear of failure can prevent them from engaging in reading. Without confidence in themselves as readers, students often disengage from any serious attempts to improve their reading.

For most adolescents the desire to feel in charge of important dimensions of their lives such as their clothes, music, and free time is an important developmental issue. We have found that when we can convincingly frame the hard work of improving reading as an avenue toward increased individual autonomy and control as well as toward an expanded repertoire of future life options, we have won more than half the battle.

Learning to independently read unfamiliar types of texts and complex texts is hard work. Unless students begin to see reading as related to their personal interests and goals and as something they can improve, they are unlikely to expend the necessary effort. For poor achievers to become more motivated and persistent, the key is seeing that their effort really does lead to success.

In developing the personal dimension of a reading apprenticeship classroom, teachers and students work together to develop new identities as readers, awareness of their own reading processes, willing persistence in the hard work of building stronger reading skills, and increased confidence for tackling new and unfamiliar kinds of texts.

Reading researchers have identified having a sense of who one is as a reader as an important aspect of motivation.[12] Especially for students who think of themselves as nonreaders or poor readers, developing a sense of *reader identity* is crucial. Teachers can create classroom routines or periodic activities that help students see themselves as readers, come to know what texts they like and don't like, identify where their strengths and weaknesses as readers lie, and articulate and monitor their own goals as developing readers. The following classroom activities can help students see themselves as readers.

Developing Reader Identity

- Write and talk with others about previous reading experiences.
- Write and talk with others about reading habits, likes, and dislikes.
- Write and talk with others about reasons for reading.
- Set and periodically check in on goals for personal reading development.

Gaining metacognitive awareness is a necessary step to gaining control of one's mental activity. Consciousness of their own thinking processes allows learners to "reflectively turn around on their own thought and action and analyze how and why their thinking achieved certain ends or failed to achieve others."[13] Moreover, knowledge of one's own thinking is like other kinds of knowledge in that it grows through experience (that is, through the metacognitive activity itself) and becomes more automatic with practice.[14]

Students find becoming conscious of their mental processes unfamiliar yet often intriguing. Here are some examples of classroom activities that assist students in thinking about their thinking.

Developing Metacognition

- Notice what is happening in your mind in a variety of everyday situations.

- Identify various thinking processes you engage in in a variety of everyday situations.

- Notice where your attention is when you read.

- Identify all the different processes going on while you read.

- Choose what thinking activities to engage in; direct and control your reading processes accordingly.

One of the paradoxes struggling or disengaged readers face is that in order to become more confident readers and to enjoy reading more, they need to become more fluent readers. Yet it is difficult to develop fluency when one doesn't feel confident and interested in reading. Our colleagues in the Academic Literacy course and in the Strategic Literacy Network have developed a variety of ways of approaching this very difficult area.

Developing Reader Fluency and Stamina

- Demonstrate that all readers, including the teacher, are developing readers and that everyone has room to grow during a lifetime of reading.

- Identify the role effort plays in the growth of reading comprehension over time; notice that effort pays off in becoming a stronger reader.

- Notice and celebrate progress as a developing reader; increase patience with yourself as a learner.

- Persist in reading even when somewhat confused or bored with a text.

- Build stamina for reading longer texts and for longer periods of time.

Another paradox teachers face in developing students' personal relationships to reading is that readers who do not feel confident about their abilities are less likely to take the risks involved in approaching new kinds of texts. Extending the range of what they can read, however, is an important way students can build their confidence as readers. Students (and their teachers) are often unaware of just how much reading they do daily. The skills, strategies, and knowledge students bring to making sense of such daily reading as notes from friends or parents, Internet Web pages, movie and music reviews, song lyrics, and computer manuals are valuable resources teachers need to invite into the classroom. Convincing students they have already mastered many text types helps build the kind of confidence they need to approach less familiar texts.

Our colleagues have used a number of activities to build such confidence and expand the range of texts students read.

Developing Reader Confidence and Range

- Bring the huge variety of different kinds of texts students read in their daily lives into the classroom.

- Investigate how students approach and make sense of these different kinds of texts.

- Connect the competencies students demonstrate in approaching these texts to the resources students will need to approach unfamiliar texts.

- Have students read, with class support, short pieces representing a wide range of unfamiliar types of texts.

- Draw attention to what students do understand when reading unfamiliar texts.

The Cognitive Dimension

The cognitive dimension of the reading apprenticeship approach focuses on increasing students' repertoire of cognitive strategies for making sense of texts (Figure 2.4). Through personal and social activities that engage students and teachers in thinking about and sharing their reading processes, the different ways readers approach reading begin to emerge. This sets the stage for learning new and perhaps more powerful ways to read. The goal of classroom work in the cognitive dimension is to expand the repertoire of strategies students can use independently to control their own reading processes, and thereby, their comprehension.

A great deal of research since the 1970s has identified and detailed many different cognitive strategies used by good readers to puzzle through a difficult text and to restore comprehension when they lose it: we discuss a number of them in this section. This research shows that these cognitive strategies can be taught to students who do not use them spontaneously on their own.[15] And once students learn these strategies and use

FIGURE 2.4

Supporting Reading Apprenticeship—The Cognitive Dimension

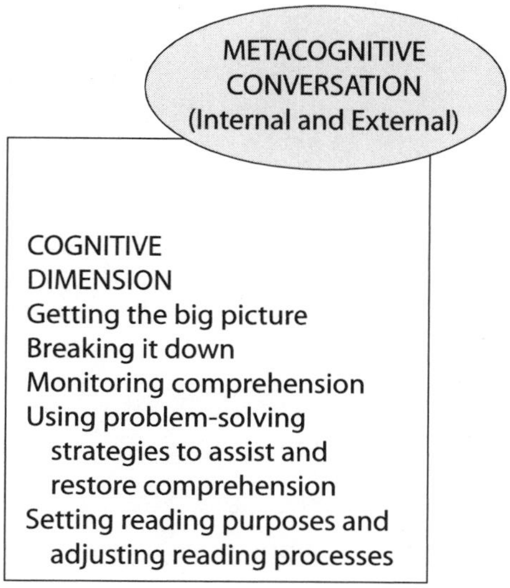

METACOGNITIVE
CONVERSATION
(Internal and External)

COGNITIVE
DIMENSION
Getting the big picture
Breaking it down
Monitoring comprehension
Using problem-solving
　strategies to assist and
　restore comprehension
Setting reading purposes and
　adjusting reading processes

them for their own reading purposes, they gain confidence and a sense of control over their reading processes and comprehension. It is important however, to integrate this strategy teaching and strategy practice into the reading of subject area texts precisely where these strategies will come in handy for students who find such reading difficult. Teaching students a disembodied set of cognitive strategies—separate from the texts that necessitate their use and without the support students need to make use of these strategies on their own—will not develop students' strength and independence as readers.

To begin with, strategies such as skimming, scanning, and reading ahead all give students a view of the whole text, even though particular aspects of it may need later clarification. Part of a strategic approach to texts is helping students live with ambiguity and confusion and helping them understand that they do not have to comprehend everything immediately. They can return to work on problem spots in the text, perhaps with some problem-solving strategies, after they get a glimpse of the whole. These strategies give students the ability to approach texts they may otherwise feel are too difficult to jump into. Teachers can model and guide students in practicing these ways of approaching difficult texts.

Getting the Big Picture

- Skim or scan texts.

- Read through ambiguity and confusion.

- Read ahead to see if confusion clears up.
- Review the big picture to check comprehension.

Researchers have also found that proficient readers break texts into comprehensible units, using a variety of strategies. Breaking down the text is a particularly useful reading strategy when comprehension fails. By rereading the problematic segment of the text, readers can often identify the *chunk* in need of closer attention and focus on just that part to restore comprehension. Our colleagues have incorporated some of these strategies for breaking down the text into their classrooms.

Breaking It Down
- Chunk texts into small segments: for example, break complex sentences into component clauses.
- Identify or clarify pronoun references and other textual connections that aid comprehension.
- Employ close reading of texts (linking interpretations to specific textual evidence).

Over two decades of research has shown that stronger readers monitor their reading, checking in with themselves to see how comprehension is progressing. Weaker readers are frequently unaware of how well they are understanding a text, but numerous intervention studies demonstrate that this critical awareness, and then control, of comprehension can be taught.[16] Here are some activities that teachers can model and guide students to carry out so they can monitor their comprehension while reading difficult texts.

Monitoring Comprehension
- Check to see whether comprehension is occurring.
- Test understanding by summarizing or paraphrasing the text or self-questioning.
- Decide whether to clarify any confusions at this time.

Researchers have found that to help developing readers make sense of what they read, it is important to help them maintain their mental engagement with texts while reading.[17] Students' engagement with and comprehension of texts is increased by activities that help them understand that reading is an active, problem-solving process to make meaning and that they must draw on all their knowledge and experiences because a good reader's whole self is involved in reading.

All of the following strategies are used by proficient readers as a way of consolidating and refining their understanding as they read and when comprehension founders.

Using Problem-Solving Strategies to Assist and Restore Comprehension

- Question texts, authors, and yourself about the text.

- Talk to the text through marginal annotations.

- Visualize what is described in the text.

- Make meaningful connections between the text and other knowledge, experiences, or texts.

- Reread sections of the text to clear up confusions

- Summarize, retell, or paraphrase texts or parts of texts.

- Represent concepts and content of texts in graphic form.

- Represent concepts and content of texts through metaphors and analogies.

- Organize and keep track of ideas in a text through graphic organizers, outlines, response logs, and notes.

Proficient readers read texts differently depending on their purposes for reading.[18] Purposes drive reading processes. On the one hand you may blitz through the television guide to find the time of a favorite show. On the other hand you may look at the offerings on every channel during a particular time slot, even consulting the movie summaries and reviews in order to make a decision about what you will watch. In the beginning, students will need to consciously set their own purposes for reading particular texts, even when those texts are assigned. Then students can begin to notice, through classroom inquiry and sharing, how purposes affect the ways readers approach particular texts.

Teachers can help students learn to let reading purposes drive their reading processes by modeling, guiding, and giving students practice.

Setting Reading Purposes and Adjusting Reading Processes

- Set goals or purposes for your reading whenever you approach a text.

- Read the same text for different purposes.

- Notice how reading purposes affect reading processes.

- Vary reading processes depending on purposes for reading.

In a reading apprenticeship classroom, students are engaged not only in practicing a variety of strategies for controlling reading processes and restoring reading comprehension but also in assessing the effects of these strategies on their own reading and reading development. Students share what they are doing to make meaning of texts. They also share *how* they are doing so, becoming more aware of their own reading strategies and serving as resources to other students in the classroom.

The Knowledge-Building Dimension

Like many other factors in reading, knowledge—whether about the world of ideas in a text, about the ways particular texts work, or about discipline-specific ways of thinking and using language—both supports reading comprehension and develops as a result of reading. In order for students to become proficient at reading to learn, they need to know something about the topics they will encounter in the text if they are to make connections to the ideas and elaborate their prior understandings. And in order for students to access different types of texts, they need to know how to read the conventions, the signposts authors leave, that direct the reader through the author's ideas. To make sense of disciplinary texts, students also need to know about the customary ways of thinking, and therefore reading, that constitute the practice of science, history, math, and literature. These different types of knowledge—knowledge about content, knowledge about texts, and knowledge about disciplinary ways of thinking—are vital resources supporting comprehension (Figure 2.5).

Research on proficient readers' mental processes has led to some key modern understandings about how the mind works, about how people think, even about what we think with. Studies conducted in the 1970s began to demonstrate how readers interact with texts, bringing their own stores of knowledge into play as they attempt to shape possible text meanings.[19] Readers do not passively absorb information from the text, but rather actively mobilize their own knowledge structures to make meaning in interaction with the text.

Readers call up whole worlds of knowledge and associations as they read, triggered by particular ideas, words, or situations. These knowledge structures are known as *schemata*. Schemata for particular networks of knowledge and information are activated as individuals read and add to their existing schemata as they encounter new information.[20] In addition, their existing schemata influence the ways they approach and make sense of texts.

Schemata, stores of knowledge about texts and about the world, are organized as networks of associations, which can be triggered by a single word. For example, the word *ball* may call up images of baseball diamonds, backstops, and bases, as well as the pitchers, batters, catchers, umps, fielders, and even sports commentators who take part in the game. Innings,

FIGURE 2.5

Supporting Reading Apprenticeship— The Knowledge-Building Dimension

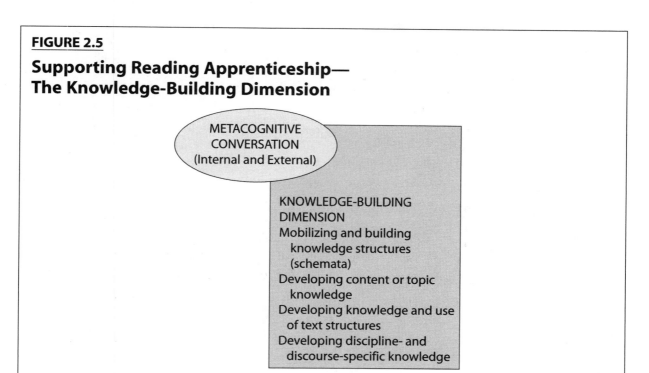

errors, random statistics about particular players, and even the smells and sounds of baseball stadiums may quickly and automatically come to mind as such images and ideas flood into consciousness. The same word, ball, may for another reader call up a competing schema: images of fancy gowns, corsages, tuxedos, limousine rides, and the blushing self-consciousness of a first prom. Proficient readers know they must relinquish any schema that proves inappropriate as they encounter further information from the text, but less experienced readers will often hold onto inappropriate images that block meaningful connections with the text.

Knowledge can be stored in other ways, as well, for example as *grammars* for particular kinds of texts. Proficient readers of children's stories will have a *story grammar* that enables them to predict what will unfold after "once upon a time."[21] Knowledge can also be stored as a *script* for an event with a well-known and predictable structure, such as a birthday party or eating out in a restaurant.[22] From experience in ordering meals in restaurants, individuals have a script for the routine of getting the host or hostess's attention, being seated and given menus, and so forth. They are therefore not surprised when a person approaches with a small pad of paper, and asks, "Have you decided yet?"

In a reading apprenticeship classroom, teachers assist students not only to activate appropriate schemata for particular texts but also to recognize that texts trigger whole networks of associated knowledge and experiences. These activities can give students necessary practice.

Mobilizing and Building Knowledge Structures (Schemata)

- Recognize the different schemata that can be triggered by a single text.
- Share the schemata individual readers bring to mind while reading a particular text.
- Identify the schemata appropriate for making sense of particular texts.
- Relinquish competing but inappropriate schemata for particular texts.

Many studies have shown that students with prior knowledge of the topics they will encounter in a text comprehend more of the text and also recall more information from it than students who lack this knowledge.[23] Because prior knowledge is such a powerful resource for comprehension, many kinds of prereading activities, such as giving students prereading guides and brief text summaries before they read the text, have been developed as ways to build schemata, thereby increasing student comprehension and retention of information. In addition, educators have developed many ways to activate the knowledge students already have about topics they are going to read about. Finally, many studies have shown that in the face of new and competing information, students relinquish their previous conceptions or ideas with great difficulty.[24] Strategies for articulating and challenging misconceptions are important if teachers are to counter the strong but incorrect theories students hold about many topics.

Teachers can use activities like these to prepare students to learn new information.

Developing Content or Topic Knowledge

- Brainstorm and share knowledge or information about the topic.
- Identify conflicting knowledge or information about the topic.
- Imagine yourself in situations similar to those that will be encountered in the text.
- Explore conceptual vocabulary that will be encountered.
- Take positions on a topic before reading about it, perhaps by writing essays on the topic before reading.
- Evaluate the fit between your prior knowledge or conception of a topic and the ideas in the text.

Although prior knowledge about the content of a text is an important resource that readers draw on to further their comprehension, it is not the only kind of knowledge they need. Knowledge about the ways different kinds of texts are structured and the ways these structures reveal the organization and interweaving of the author's ideas has also been shown to influence comprehension and memory.[25] Proficient readers use their awareness of text structure to understand the key points of a text, and when they report what they recall, their summaries reflect the text organization. Less experienced readers, apparently unaware of text structures, have difficulty organizing and prioritizing text information. In our work with urban secondary students we often see students who can follow a typical narrative but are bewildered by expository text structures. Expository texts often rely on scientific discourse, characterized by complex sentences containing multiple embedded clauses, verbs that have been turned into nouns standing for large disciplinary concepts, and Latin and Greek derived vocabularies. Yet ample research shows that when students are taught to identify text structures through the use of such supports as graphic organizers or text previewing, their comprehension increases.[26]

In the knowledge-building dimension of reading apprenticeship classrooms, teachers can assist students with activities like these.

Developing Knowledge and Use of Text Structures

- Identify the ways particular texts are structured.

- Notice patterns in structure across texts of similar kinds.

- Identify the particular kinds of language used in particular kinds of texts.

- Identify roots, prefixes, and suffixes of Latin and Greek derived words often encountered in expository texts.

- Create word families associated with particular ideas or subject areas.

- Use text organization and structure to assist in comprehension of particular texts.

- Preview a text to build a schema for it; notice structural markers such as headings, subheadings, and illustrations.

- Notice that particular words or phrases signal that the text is heading in a particular direction.

- Use signal words and phrases to aid comprehension and to predict the direction particular texts will take next.

Little has yet been studied about effective ways to integrate into reading instruction knowledge about customary ways of thinking and using language that characterize discourse in particular academic disciplines.[27] Despite the relative lack of research, we feel students need to understand the specific "habits of mind" characteristic of particular academic disciplines[28] in order to make sense of academic texts. We have observed how important it is for our own students to know how particular texts are functioning in the world, what enterprise these texts serve, and what social practices the texts are contributing to. Knowing about topics and text structures alone does not help students who are bewildered by the larger *sense* of a text as a disciplinary enterprise. For example, students are often unaware that scientific activity is motivated by the enterprise of explanation or discovery or that history is an enterprise devoted to interpretation and explanation of events or that the study of literature can be understood as an aesthetic exploration of the human condition.

Discipline-specific knowledge is related to the more general idea of communicative competence—competence in producing and comprehending particular forms of language, or discourse—which develops in particular social settings. In the past two decades, research in the varied fields of linguistics, social psychology, cognitive science, anthropology, and education has illustrated how proficient readers and writers of particular texts acquire not just the component skills or processes needed to read and write but the ways of participating in literacy activities valued by particular communities of readers and writers.[29] They learn specific "ways with words"[30] by actively participating in reading or writing in the company and with the guidance of more skilled practitioners.

Authors who write within the practice and language conventions of a discipline often assume that readers have an appreciation and understanding of that discipline's ways of thinking. Specialized ways of thinking have associated specialized ways of using language, which we call *disciplinary ways with words*. In our work in the Academic Literacy course and with our broader network of secondary teachers, we have been exploring ways to help students build their knowledge of text structures and of the ways with words and ways of thinking that are characteristic of different disciplines. These types of knowledge are particularly important when educators hope to apprentice student readers to academic reading, yet they have rarely been included in subject area teaching. We believe that teaching students about the text structures of disciplinary text and the disciplinary enterprise these texts mirror will enable students to "crack the codes"[31] of academic texts in order to become more successful and ultimately more independent learners.

Teachers can help students acquire disciplinary and discourse-specific knowledge by making their own disciplinary habits of mind visible to students through think-alouds and class discussion, helping to demystify the hidden codes—the ways of using language, the conventions of form, and the larger questions and standards of inquiry and evidence—that count in particular disciplines. Moreover, they can engage students in classroom activities such as these.

Developing Discipline- and Discourse-Specific Knowledge

- Identify the possible purposes that the authors of particular texts may have had in creating these texts.

- Identify the possible audiences particular texts seem to be addressing.

- Identify the functions particular texts serve in particular circumstances.

- Explore the large questions, purposes, and habits of mind that characterize specific academic disciplines.

- Inquire into the ways texts function in particular disciplines.

- Identify the particular ways of using language associated with particular academic disciplines.

In Part Two, we bring the reading apprenticeship approach to life through portraits of classroom practice illustrating the metacognitive conversation and each of the four dimensions. We also present lessons and specific assignments from Academic Literacy and the classrooms of our colleagues in the Strategic Literacy Initiative. Because these are real classrooms, their activities resist neat categorization into one or the other of the interacting dimensions of the reading apprenticeship approach, though we try, for the sake of exposition, to do so. Nevertheless, the fact that the dimensions overlap in our approach is an important part of the picture we want to illustrate. Areas of classroom life overlap, activities serve multiple purposes, and we are always doing more, as we construct teaching and learning in the classroom, than may at first be obvious. We hope that what emerges in these portraits of practice is a vision of classrooms in which young people are engaged, motivated, and clearly gaining power, knowledge, and independence as readers.

Notes

1. R. Ruddell and N. Unrau, "Reading as a Meaning-Construction Process: The Reader, the Text, and the Teacher," in R. Ruddell, M. Ruddell, and H. Singer (eds.), *Theoretical Models and Processes of Reading* (Newark: Del.: International Reading Association, 1994).

2. J. J. Pikulski, *Improving Reading Achievement: Major Instructional Considerations for the Primary Grades,* paper presented at the Commissioner's

Reading Day Statewide Conference, Austin, Tex., Feb. 25, 1998, cited in D. R. Reutzel and R. B. Cooter Jr., *Balanced Reading Strategies and Practices* (Upper Saddle River, N.J.: Prentice Hall, 1999), p. 147.

3. See for example, J. F. Baumann and A. M. Duffy, *Engaged Reading for Pleasure and Learning: A Report from the National Reading Research Center* (Athens, Ga.: National Reading Research Center, 1997).

4. L. S. Vygotsky, *Thought and Language,* rev. ed., A. Kozulin, trans. and ed. (Cambridge, Mass.: MIT Press, 1986); L. S. Vygotsky, *Mind in Society* (Cambridge, Mass.: Harvard University Press, 1978).

5. See, for example, J. Brown, A. Collins, and P. Deguid, "Situated Cognition and the Culture of Learning," *Educational Researcher,* 1989, *18*(1), 32–42; A. Collins, J. S. Brown, and S. E. Newman, "Cognitive Apprenticeship: Teaching the Craft of Reading, Writing, and Mathematics," in L. B. Resnick (ed.), *Knowing, Learning and Instruction: Essays in Honor of Robert Glaser* (Hillsdale, N.J.: Erlbaum, 1989); J. Lave and E. Wenger, *Situated Learning: Legitimate Peripheral Participation* (Cambridge, England: Cambridge University Press, 1991); C. Lee, "A Culturally Based Cognitive Apprenticeship: Teaching African American High School Students Skills in Literary Interpretation," *Reading Research Quarterly,* 1995, *30*(4), 608–630; B. Rogoff, *Apprenticeship in Thinking: Cognitive Development in Social Context* (New York: Oxford University Press, 1990); B. Rogoff and J. Lave, *Everyday Cognition: Its Development in Social Context* (Cambridge, Mass.: Harvard University Press, 1984).

6. D. Rose, *Apprenticeship and Exploration: A New Approach to Literacy Instruction,* adapted from a speech delivered at the May 1994 meeting of the International Reading Association (New York: Scholastic, 1995).

7. L. Kucan and I. Beck, "Thinking Aloud and Reading Comprehension Research: Inquiry, Instruction, and Social Interaction," *Review of Educational Research,* 1997, *67*(3), 271–299; P. D. Pearson and L. Fielding, "Balancing Authenticity and Strategy Awareness in Comprehension Instruction" ([http://www.ed-web3.educ.msu.edu/cspds/pdppaper/balacin.htm], 1998).

8. J. H. Flavell, "Metacognitive Dimensions of Problem-Solving," in L. B. Resnick (ed.), *The Nature of Intelligence* (Hillsdale, N.J.: Erlbaum, 1976).

9. See, for example, L. S. Shulman, "Just in Case: Reflections on Learning from Experience," in J. Colbert, P. Dresberg, and K. Trimble (eds.), *The Case for Education: Contemporary Approaches for Using Case Methods* (Needham Heights, Mass.: Allyn & Bacon, 1986).

10. L. Steinberg, *Beyond the Classroom: Why School Reform Has Failed and What Parents Need to Do* (New York: Simon & Schuster, 1996).

11. S. Paris, M. Lipson, and K. Wixson, "Becoming a Strategic Reader," in Ruddell, Ruddell, and Singer, *Theoretical Models and Processes of Reading.*

12. Baumann and Duffy, *Engaged Reading.*

13. Shulman, "Just in Case," p. 210.

14. See, for example, Flavell, "Metacognitive Dimensions of Problem-Solving."

15. I. L. Beck, "Improving Practice Through Understanding Reading," in L. B. Resnick and L. E. Klopfer (eds.), *Toward the Thinking Curriculum: Current Cognitive Research,* 1989 ASCD Yearbook (Alexandria, Va.: Association for Supervision and Curriculum Development, 1989); J. Fitzgerald, "English-as-a-Second-Language Learners' Cognitive Reading Processes: A Review of Research in the United States," *Review of Educational Research,* 1995, *65*(2), 145–190; Pearson, and Fielding, "Balancing Authenticity and Strategy Awareness."

16. R. Garner, "Metacognition and Executive Control"; A. L. Brown, A. Palincsar, and B. Armbruster, "Instructing Comprehension-Fostering Activities in Interactive Learning Situations," in Ruddell, Ruddell, and Singer, *Theoretical Models and Processes of Reading.*

17. Baumann and Duffy, *Engaged Reading;* J. T. Guthrie and A. Wigfield (eds.), *Reading Engagement: Motivating Readers Through Integrated Instruction* (Newark, Del.: International Reading Association, 1997; G. Mathewson, "Model of Attitude Influence upon Reading and Learning to Read," in Ruddell, Ruddell, and Singer, *Theoretical Models and Processes of Reading;* P. S. Bristow, "Are Poor Readers Passive Readers? Some Evidence, Possible Explanations, and Potential Solutions." *The Reading Teacher,* Dec. 1985, pp. 318–325."

18. W. Blanton, K. Wood, and G. Moorman, "The Role of Purpose in Reading Instruction," *The Reading Teacher,* 1990, *43,* 486–493.

19. R. Anderson, "Role of the Reader's Schema in Comprehension, Learning, and Memory," in Ruddell, Ruddell, and Singer, *Theoretical Models and Processes of Reading;* D. Pearson and K. Camperell, "Comprehension of Text Structures," in Ruddell, Ruddell, and Singer, *Theoretical Models and Processes of Reading.*

20. Anderson, "Role of the Reader's Schema"; J. Bransford, "Schema Activation and Schema Acquisition," in Ruddell, Ruddell, and Singer, *Theoretical Models and Processes of Reading;* S. Simonsen and H. Singer, "Improving Reading Instruction in the Content Areas," in J. Samuels and A. Farstrup (eds.), *What Research Has to Say About Reading Instruction,* 2nd ed. (Newark, Del.: International Reading Association, 1992).

21. Pearson and Camperell, "Comprehension of Text Structures."

22. Anderson, "Role of the Reader's Schema."

23. G. H. Bower, "Experiments on Story Understanding and Recall," *Quarterly Journal of Experimental Psychology 28,* 511–534, 1976; Pearson and Camperell, "Comprehension of Text Structures."

24. Simonsen and Singer, "Improving Reading Instruction in the Content Areas." Bransford, "Schema Activation and Schema Acquisition."

25. I. Beck, R. Omanson, and M. McKeown, "An Instructional Redesign of Reading Lessons: Effects on Comprehension," *Reading Research Quarterly,* 1982, *17,* 462–481; S. Berkowitz, "Effects of Instruction in Text Organization on Sixth-Grade Students' Memory for Expository Reading," *Reading Research Quarterly,* 1986, *21,* 161–178; B. Taylor, "Text Structure, Comprehension, and Recall," in Samuels and Farstrup, *What Research Has to Say About Reading Instruction.*

26. Pearson and Camperell, "Comprehension of Text Structures."

27. For examples of studies that might (rather loosely) be classified as discourse studies, see P. L. Courts, *Multicultural Literacies: Dialect, Discourse, and Diversity* (New York: Peter Lang, 1997).; B. Cope and M. Kalantzis, *The Powers of Literacy* (Pittsburgh, Pa.: University of Pittsburgh Press, 1993); J. Gee, *The Social Mind: Language, Ideology, and Social Practice* (New York: Bergin & Garvey, 1992); A. Luke and P. Gilbert, *Literacy in Contexts: Australian Perspectives and Issues* (Sydney: Allen & Unwin, 1993); P. Rabinowitz and M. Smith, *Authorizing Readers: Resistance and Respect in the Teaching of Literature* (New York: Teachers College Press, 1998); P. Rabinowitz, *Before Reading: Narrative Conventions and the Politics of Interpretation* (Ithaca, N.Y.: Cornell University Press, 1987).

28. G. Wiggins, "Coaching Habits of Mind: Pursuing Essential Questions in the Classroom." *Horace, 5*(5), June 1989.

29. D. Bartholomae, "Inventing the University," in M. Rose, *When a Writer Can't Write: Studies in Writer's Block and Other Composing Process Problems* (New York: Guilford Press, 1985); Lee, "A Culturally Based Cognitive Apprenticeship"; Courts, *Multicultural Literacies;* Rabinowitz and Smith, *Authorizing Readers;* J. Scott, *Science and Language Links: Classroom Implications* (Portsmouth, N.H.: Heinemann, 1993); S. Michaels, M. C. O'Connor, and J. Richards, *Literacy as Reasoning Within Multiple Discourses: Implications for Policy and Educational Reform,* presentation to the Council of Chief State School Officers, 1990 Summer Institute); S. S. Wineburg, "On the Reading of Historical Texts: Notes on the Breach Between School and Academy," *American Educational Research Journal,* 1991, *28*(3), 495–519.

30. S. B. Heath, *Ways with Words: Language, Life and Work in Communities and Classrooms* (Cambridge, England: Cambridge University Press, 1983).

31. Courts, *Multicultural Literacies;* L. D. Delpit, *Other People's Children: Cultural Conflict in the Classroom* (New York: New Press, 1995).

Part Two

Reading Apprenticeship in the Classroom

Chapter 3
Developing Academic Literacy

I would also like to say that since I've been in this class and you've been stressing reading, it's become a custom to me. What I mean is like for example now when I go out I take my SSR book most of the time instead of my Walkman.

A ninth-grade student

FROM OCTOBER 1996 to May 1997, a diverse group of ninth-grade students—the entire freshman class at San Francisco's Thurgood Marshall Academic High School—improved their reading comprehension by an average of two years, as measured on a nationally normed standardized reading test. These gains were consistent across all ethnic groups and across the four different teachers' classrooms in which an innovative course called Academic Literacy was taught. These test score gains were accompanied by impressive changes in students' reading attitudes and habits. After comparing their responses on a reading survey conducted in October to their responses to the same survey in May (see Appendix B), many students expressed pride and surprise about the changes they saw in themselves, reporting, for example, "I am surprised because my whole attitude toward reading has changed since I was in this class and that is the honest to God truth," and "I feel proud of myself as a reader. I really did grow."

This is a rare success story for an urban public high school. Its seeds were planted when the two authors of this book who are teachers at Thurgood Marshall and other Marshall teachers decided to address a challenge familiar to many middle and high school teachers across the United States: a majority of our freshman students seemed unable to independently read and understand the variety of texts assigned in their history, science, English, and math classes. One of us, Christine Cziko, as head of the English Department during the creation of the Academic Literacy course, took the lead in working with WestEd's SLI staff to conceptualize, design, and implement the course on-site. One of us, Lori Hurwitz, was a first-year teacher when this course was first taught and is still teaching the course.

At the time our team of teachers decided to address this problem, Thurgood Marshall Academic High School, which had opened in the fall of 1994, was still a relatively new school. Staff were still actively involved in creating the school's identity and discovering ways to better serve the student body. The school's mission—to serve both as a neighborhood school for one of San Francisco's poorest communities and, at the same time, as a school with a focus on mathematics, science, and technology that promised to prepare all its students for entry into college—created a high-stakes challenge for staff, students, and parents alike.

Students are accepted by lottery, although students in the school's immediate neighborhood are offered preferential enrollment. The school's only entrance requirement is that a family member sign a request for the student to attend. Students are ethnically diverse: African Americans represent about 30 percent of the student body, Latinos another 25 percent, Chinese American students around 24 percent, and Filipino American and other nonwhite students about 8 percent each. There are also small numbers of Japanese American, white, and American Indian students. ELL (English language learner) students represent about 13 percent of the population, and EDY (educationally disadvantaged youth) students (those falling below the fortieth percentile on either the reading or math subtest of the CTBS (Comprehensive Test of Basic Skills), 43 percent.

Although the students were told before entering Thurgood Marshall that the word *academic* in the school's name meant they would be expected to work hard, many of them were unprepared for the demands of a curriculum geared to prepare them to succeed at a four-year college. During the first two years of the school's operations, we and many of our colleagues had noticed that a high number of our students were having difficulty getting through heavy reading requirements that our curriculum demanded. Although we tried a variety of strategies to promote greater success, including creating extensive interdisciplinary community-based projects, which did increase students' academic engagement, many students still had grades of D or F or took an incomplete (I) in at least one of their classes. A large percentage were earning less than a 2.0 grade point average.

For these students, receiving low grades in this new academic high school underscored their vision of themselves as not academically inclined. Students told interviewers that they saw themselves as somehow significantly different from their peers who "got it," academically speaking. A closer examination revealed that this sense of academic inadequacy was rooted in a history of reading struggles.

Creating Academic Literacy

As these issues surrounding students' academic underachievement were coming into sharper focus for our school community, a team of several of us from the English and Social Science Departments had begun participating in the SLI. Ideas, research, and classroom strategies we were learning about and developing in this professional literacy network formed the nucleus of the new Academic Literacy course. The goal of Academic Literacy was to prepare our students to become more confident and competent in reading the kinds of texts they would be assigned in different disciplines throughout the rest of their high school classes and beyond.

Although we created the Academic Literacy course to meet a pressing need, we knew that ultimately the ideas and approaches to reading subject area texts that we would focus on in this stand-alone course would need to be embedded in courses across the curriculum. In order to begin building a focus on reading across the curriculum, we made a special effort to involve two social studies teachers as part of the teaching team for the pilot year of Academic Literacy, along with the two of us who taught English.

One of the most important decisions our school community made about Academic Literacy was to require it for all freshmen. We believed strongly that all freshmen could benefit from becoming more conscious of the mental strategies involved in reading different types of texts. We also believed that diverse readers would learn from each other, and we did not want to establish a school culture in which only the so-called slow students improved their reading abilities and the others did not. In addition, we wanted to pilot powerful approaches to helping students become more expert readers across the curriculum, and we believed the entire faculty would more likely support this effort if Academic Literacy was a course for all students, not just for those considered most at risk.

Although we had the crucial and very strong support of our principal and many other faculty, not all our colleagues liked the idea of this new *mandatory elective* course. One broadly held concern was that, given existing school requirements, Academic Literacy would either displace another course or eliminate precious slots for electives. This concern proved well-founded, and these trade-offs remain one of the difficulties of offering the course. Some teachers also expressed fears that a literacy class would not be engaging enough to make students take it seriously. Other important faculty concerns had to do with the absence of readily available and adaptable curriculum and assessment tools for such a course. Those of us committed to creating the course persuaded our colleagues that we were ready to take on the job of working with the Strategic Literacy Initiative (SLI) staff to create the curriculum and to scout for appropriate materials and assessment tools over the summer.

In addition, all four of us on the Academic Literacy teaching team made a commitment to meet each week for an hour after school to do the continual updating, refining, and in some cases further creating of the curriculum as we progressed through the pilot year. During the summer before our pilot year, and throughout the year as we pulled together materials for these units, we looked for short text selections that would (1) portray different views of the role of reading in people's lives; (2) give students practice with a variety of disciplinary readings in, for example, science, history, and literature; and (3) be appropriately challenging, that is, not so difficult that students could not read them at all but difficult enough so that students would be motivated to use some of the new strategies they were learning.

In responding to faculty concerns about the new course we had also promised to present updates on course progress, to discuss any other faculty issues, and to report on student achievement data at faculty meetings. At the beginning of the next school year we were delighted to be able to announce the strong gains the ninth-grade students had made both in reading achievement and in habits and attitudes (see Appendix B). Later that fall we also met with our former Academic Literacy students—now tenth graders—to tell them about the reading gains their whole class had made. And we have continued to work with SLI staff to track these students' test scores (using the same assessment instrument throughout). We are happy to say that the gains the students made in that pilot year of Academic Literacy are holding as they move into their senior year.

Curriculum

Academic Literacy has been conceived as a yearlong course to help incoming ninth graders become higher-level, strategic readers. It is focused on helping them become engaged, fluent, and competent readers of the various types of texts necessary for their success across disciplines in high school, in postsecondary education, in employment, and in everyday life.

The course is designed as an inquiry into reading, with teachers as master readers and students as their apprentices. More specifically, we designed the course around a set of learning goals, or competencies (see Exhibit 3.1), that grew out of our attempts to synthesize the broad field of reading research and find ways to apply research findings to the particular literacy learning and developmental needs of adolescents.

Students in the course were invited into a yearlong inquiry that would explore what reading is and what proficient readers do when they read. They signed off on class guidelines that outlined what they were expected to achieve and how the class would be conducted (Exhibit 3.2). They were encouraged to get to know themselves as readers and to build their motivation for reading, exploring questions such as:

What are my characteristics as a reader?

What strategies do I use as I read?

What roles does reading serve in people's personal and public lives?

What roles will reading play in my future education and career goals?

What goals do I want to set and work toward to help myself develop as a reader?

Our students encountered and revisited these questions through a series of units and activities designed to engage them in ideas, strategies, and practices that demystified disciplinary reading and apprenticed them as academic readers.

During the pilot year of the Academic Literacy course, we taught three units: Reading Self and Society, Reading Media, and Reading History. Now we have developed and piloted a fourth unit, Reading Science and Technology.

Unit One: Reading Self and Society. In the twelve-week Reading Self and Society unit, students focus on inquiry into the personal and public worlds of reading through guided reflection into their own and others' reading histories and experiences. While conducting personal inquiries into their own reading, they read narratives from authors such as Malcolm X, Claude Brown, Frederick Douglass, and Maxine Hong Kingston, taking the points of view of these authors to answer the question, Why read?

Perhaps the most important part of this first unit is that students begin *silent sustained reading* (SSR) of self-chosen books. In SSR, students read a book of their choice for twenty to twenty-five minutes at least twice a week. Although we are aware that some reading educators caution teachers to make all student-chosen reading free and voluntary, we reasoned

EXHIBIT 3.1

Academic Literacy: Student Competencies

Area of Competency	Examples of What Students Will Know and Be Able to Do
Personal dimension	• Become increasingly aware of preferences, habits, processes, and growth as readers • Set goals for purposeful engagement with reading • Increase reading fluency • Increase confidence, risk taking, focus, and persistence in reading
Social dimension	• Share confusions about texts with others • Share successful processes and approaches to understanding texts with others • Participate in small- and large-group discussions about reading and texts • Appreciate alternative points of view
Cognitive dimension	• Monitor comprehension • Ask different types of questions of the text • Summarize the text • Clarify understanding of the text by rereading, searching for context clues, continuing to read, and tolerating uncertainty • Make predictions based on the content or structure of the text
Knowledge-building dimension: Content	• Use a variety of strategies to access and interpret information in textbooks and other course materials • Preread texts and generate questions • Use graphic organizers to organize and build knowledge structures • Identify and access relevant knowledge and experiences
Knowledge-building dimension: Texts	• Identify text features such as signal words, structure, and specialized vocabulary • Approach novel words strategically, using prior experience, context, and structural clues to meaning • Identify and use structural signal words and phrases
Knowledge-building dimension: Disciplines and discourses	• Recognize the large questions, purposes, and habits of mind that characterize specific academic disciplines • View texts as constructed artifacts that are addressed to readers familiar with the worlds they represent • Become familiar with specialized vocabulary, semantics, concepts, phrases, idioms of different disciplines and discourses
Writing	• Write from a particular point of view • Respond to text excerpts • Paraphrase texts • Compose a variety of texts for different purposes (interviews, reflections, summaries, letters, descriptions, logs, commercials, journals, posters, oral presentations)
Research	• Categorize, synthesize, and organize information from texts • Evaluate information sources • Identify primary and secondary sources • Interpret primary source documents

<u>**EXHIBIT 3.2**</u>
Academic Literacy: Class Guidelines

Thurgood Marshall Academic H.S.   **Fall 1997**

Academic Literacy

This is a course about reading. Its goal is to help you become engaged, fluent, and competent readers of the variety of texts that you will have to understand in your personal, academic, and professional lives.

In Unit I, *Reading Self and Society,* we will explore the nature of reading. What is reading? What is the role of reading in personal and public life? What are the qualities of successful readers, and what strategies do they use? What is the connection between reading competency and your own educational and professional goals?

You will use Silent Sustained Reading (SSR) time to increase fluency and help you learn how to pick books that you enjoy. You will also keep an SSR log to become more aware of your reading strengths and weaknesses. You will practice using different thinking strategies to help you understand different kinds of reading materials.

You will learn how to focus your attention, deal with distractions, and organize your time in order to become a more effective learner. The skills, habits, and understandings you gain from this course will help you in all of your other classes.

Behavior Expectations

1. The Thurgood Marshall Way will be practiced in this class.
2. Disrespect toward any member of the class will not be tolerated.
3. Be on time to class and ready to participate.
4. Grades—Everything Counts:
   SSR in books of choice and SSR Logs
   Unit learning logs and other written assignments
   Book projects and presentations
   Homework, tests, and quizzes
   Participation, preparation, and cooperation

If you have any problems or questions I encourage you to make an appointment to see me after class or during lunch. I will help you in any way that I can.   Ms. Cziko

....

I have read and understand the above class guidelines.

_____   _____

Student's Signature   Parent/Guardian's Signature that students would continue to avoid reading as long as they were not held accountable for it. Students are expected to read at least two hundred pages each month, maintain a reflective reading log, write reflective letters about their reading to the teacher, and design a project or presentation about their book. Far from discouraging students from reading, the seriousness with which SSR is treated soon communicates to students the importance of reading and has the effect of reengaging those who had stopped reading as they moved into middle school. (See Appendix A for a more detailed outline of Unit One.)

Unit Two: Reading Media. The second unit of Academic Literacy, Reading Media, is a six-week unit that introduces students to commercials as visual texts similar to printed texts they have been exposed to. Students are taught to *investigate texts* as authors' creations that are devised or constructed in particular times and places and with specific purposes, intended audiences, and points of view. Students learn about visual metaphors, symbolism, persuasive argument, key messages, casting, storyboard sketching, production notes, and targeted audiences. They form advertising production teams to create their own commercials.

Unit Three: Reading History. The third unit, Reading History, which we extended in the first year into a very long (sixteen-week) unit, is designed to help students put their personal experiences in a historical context through understanding modern expressions of totalitarianism and intergroup aggression. Students learn to use a set of strategies for reading subject area textbooks and also primary source documents.

Unit Four: Reading Science and Technology. In this unit, created and piloted for the first time in spring 1999, students use strategies for reading science textbooks and primary source documents. They explore and report on a variety of texts including scientific explanations of natural disasters such as earthquakes, tornadoes, hurricans, and tidal waves.

Key instructional strategies employed in all four of the units are silent sustained reading (SSR), reciprocal teaching (RT) and its components (questioning, clarifying, summarizing, predicting), and explicit instruction in self-monitoring and cognitive strategies that facilitate reading a variety of texts. Throughout the course, students reflected on their reading and learning processes through classroom discussions as well as in various kinds of written assignments, including learning logs, double-entry journals, letters, and essays.

As this book goes to press, we are continuing to develop and refine the Academic Literacy curriculum. Teachers in other schools participating in the Strategic Literacy Network are beginning to adapt ideas from Academic Literacy as they plan and implement similar courses at their schools. The key ideas underlying the course—engaging students in an inquiry into reading and developing reading apprenticeships through a variety of course activities and routines—continue to shape and reshape the curriculum at Thurgood Marshall and at schools that are adapting and expanding the ideas developing there.

In the following three chapters, Academic Literacy teachers Christine Cziko and Lori Hurwitz describe how the desired changes in students' reading habits, attitudes, and skills developed.

Chapter 4

Motivating Students to Take Control of Their Reading

IN THE ACADEMIC LITERACY course at Thurgood Marshall Academic High School, we sought to develop classrooms that fostered both the sense of community necessary to support students' engagement with reading and the development of students' individual identities and motivations as readers. The following examination of our work in these social and personal dimensions of reading apprenticeship presents both our rationales for various activities and instructions for carrying out some of those activities.

The Social Dimension

To those of us designing the Academic Literacy course, it was clear from the start that without students' active participation, we could not know how best to help them become more competent readers. We needed them to tell us what was going on in their minds when they were reading—where they got stuck, what was confusing, what seemed easy and what did not. We had to create the sense that students and teacher formed a *community of readers* committed to a collaborative inquiry aimed at improving their reading. This meant making sure that students felt it was not just okay but *cool* to be part of this community.

Again and again, we made the point that in the course of their school, professional, and recreational lives, all individuals would encounter texts that they would find easy to understand and all would encounter texts that would confound them. We explained that reading was not a magic skill that you either had or did not have. Rather reading as we understood it was an ongoing process of problem solving, and some of the problems posed by a text would be greater than others. But we assured students that working together with each other and the teacher, they could solve problems of understanding as they read. They could learn strategies, skills, and habits that would help them become more engaged, fluent, and competent readers.

They needed a common language for that inquiry. Early on in the course, we introduced them to words like *fluency, competence, engaged,* and *schema,* explaining in easily accessible language the research behind these concepts. As one of our teachers noted, "We treated students like real partners, and they seemed to like knowing that we were doing what the 'experts said' would make a difference in their reading." We gave students the following list of simplified definitions as a handout to keep in their learning logs to reference throughout the course.

Terms and Definitions for Academic Literacy Students

- Metacognition: *a conscious examination of what you are understanding and what you are not understanding while you are reading or thinking*

- Schema: *what you already know before you try to read or learn something new*

- Engagement: *a connection to something*

- Fluency: *the ability to do something so quickly and easily that you hardly have to think about it*

- Competency: *skill in something*

- Text: *anything that communicates using language (written or oral)*

- Chunking: *breaking up sentences into pieces small enough for you to understand*

- Strategy: *a plan of action*

- Summarizing: *deciding what is most important in a text and putting it in your own words*

- Paraphrasing: *putting ideas in a text into your own words*

It's Cool to Be Confused

From long experience we understood the lengths to which students would go in order to avoid humiliation in front of their peers. They would do virtually anything to hide what they perceived to be their own inadequacies.

If we hoped to help them become self-directed, strategic readers, we would have to find a way for them to feel safe voicing confusion about what they were reading.

Throughout the first weeks of the course, we emphasized the value of talking about what one did not understand. We gave students extra credit for sharing their confusion and questions. In fact the more explicit they could be about *where* in a text they got lost or *why* they thought something was difficult for them to understand, the more credit they received. As this idea took hold and students were praised for discussing their reading difficulties, we noticed a change in many of them. As one of our colleagues put it, "It was as if all the energy they had put into hiding their sense of failure could now go into trying to understand what they were reading— or at least into understanding where they were getting lost or what it was that confused them."

To make it clear to our students that they were not the only people who could have difficulty with certain texts, we invited them to bring to class any texts they felt confident reading but thought might confuse us. Most often they brought song lyrics and sometimes computer manuals. Listening to their teachers trying to make sense of rap music or technical manuals by *thinking aloud* (verbalizing their process of trying to make sense of texts) in front of the class resulted in predictable hilarity. But this kind of modeling also underscored the point that successful reading requires an understanding of how language is used differently and conveys different content in different contexts. It also subtly reminded students that they probably had more reading expertise—with certain types of texts, whose language, content, and "rules" they already knew—than they might have thought.

This exercise allows teachers to experience the frustration of trying to unlock a door to which one has no key—a feeling students often have when trying to read academic texts. At the same time, it allows students to recognize and enjoy their own expertise as readers of particular types of texts. By first modeling our own reading process through the practice of thinking aloud and then helping students learn how to do their own *think-alouds,* we and our students began to have conversations about our reading processes. The focus of these conversations was on *how* individuals attempted, with varying degrees of success, to make sense of a variety of texts. These conversations were essential because they allowed students to share both problems with and solutions to the complex process of making meaning from written texts.

Reading Happens in Your Mind

Now I know you can be sitting reading words but not reading anything or maybe reading but just not understanding.

The starting point for our inquiry into reading processes was the basic but essential question, What is reading? Most students responded to this query based on their experiences of learning to read in earlier grades. "Well, it's simple," said one. "Reading is saying the words you see when you look at a page with words." Our job, as master readers, was to help them expand this understanding of reading. We probed these simple views of reading, asking for example whether a person who could say all the words on a page but could not tell you anything about what he had read had really *read* the page. As these discussions developed, many students recognized their own behavior and could describe what we came to call *reading with your mouth* as opposed to *reading with your mind.*

When a person is reading a text with their mouth and lips, and their mind is not focusing on this certain text, they're not reading. Reading is reading the text in your head. For example, when I was reading my SSR book, I read with my lips, but my head was thinking about what I should eat later, and the book was about murder.

Building on the understanding that reading involves mental processes of which a reader can be explicitly aware and therefore can control, we introduced the course's most important practice: thinking about thinking, or metacognition.

Metacognition: Thinking About Thinking

Anyone who has worked with adolescents knows that they are often intensely self-absorbed, consumed with questions of individual identity and of their place within their peer group. We realized that we could use this self-interest to get students thinking about their own reading processes. Self-absorption was our ally as students became increasingly motivated to uncover how and what they thought as they read and to compare their thoughts and thinking processes to those of their friends.

Getting on the Metacognitive Bus

Even with students' natural interest in themselves and each other, we found many of them had difficulty initially in grasping the concept of metacognition. We had students spend a good deal of time working with the idea of thinking about thinking as a community (the external conversation about metacognition) before we asked them to describe their individual metacognitive processes (the internal conversation). As we searched for anecdotes and analogies that would help clarify metacognition in a tangible way, one teacher came up with the idea of the *metacognitive bus*.

> *I put two chairs in the front of the classroom, positioned like seats one in back of the other on a bus. I sat down in the first chair and pretended I was trying to read but kept getting distracted every time someone new got on the bus. I told the students, "OK, that's me reading." Then I left the book in the first chair and moved to the second chair. "Here's me watching myself get distracted," I told my students. Then I started talking as though I was reporting what the "me with the book" was doing, making comments like, "Oh, there you go again, you're checking out all the cute ones. Oh, yeah, aren't you supposed to be finishing reading that story for Ms. Hurwitz's class? Well, so, you say it's boring? Well, what are you gonna do—flunk the class?" "That," I told them, "is me being metacognitive."*

Once our students started to be comfortable thinking about thinking, we began to guide more targeted discussions of the reading process. As students read a variety of texts, we began asking them to focus on specific questions about how they read, for example:

How do you know when your understanding is breaking down?

Can you point to certain places in a text where you tend to "lose it"?

How do you get back on track when you begin to notice that you are "not getting it"?

As students became more able to see and describe their reading processes and problems, we gave students a handout that introduced the following ideas about what to do when you find yourself confused while reading a text.

Steps for Clarifying Confusion While Reading
- *Ignore the unclear part and read on to see if it gets clearer.*
- *Reread the unclear part.*
- *Reread the sentence(s) before the unclear part.*
- *Try to connect the unclear part to something you already know.*

The Personal Dimension

> *I didn't crack a book unless it was necessary in middle school. Before, I just read whatever I was supposed to read. And then Ms. Cziko helped me pick out books I like to read—I like mysteries, and books set in the '70s and '80s. I guess because I know what I like, I like to read more.*

One of the most striking changes in the Academic Literacy students from the beginning of their ninth-grade year to the end was the change in how they viewed their relationships to reading. When we first asked students if they read at home for pleasure, most responded with a resounding no! By the end of the course a majority of these same students described themselves as liking to read.

Why Read?

Working with the Strategic Literacy Initiative staff, we had designed the first unit of the course, Reading Self and Society, to help students explore the why read question in multiple ways and begin to develop a unique sense of themselves as readers, their *reader identity*. It was clear to us that unless students could develop their own authentic reasons for reading, there was very little chance that anything they learned in Academic Literacy would have a lasting impact.

Toward this end, we discussed with students the question of the relationship between literacy and power in our society. They read excerpts from autobiographies, poetry, and fiction in which the authors addressed the why read question. They then discussed how reading had enriched these peoples' lives, sometimes role playing conversations in which the various authors or their characters discussed why they read.

We knew that it was very important for our ethnically diverse students to read powerful testimonies about the importance of reading from people with whom they could identify. For that reason we chose texts from a diverse group of authors, including Frederick Douglass, Emily Dickinson, Maxine Hong Kingston, Malcolm X, and Rudolpho Anaya (see the Unit One outline in Appendix A for a full list). The writings of Malcolm X proved particularly compelling for many of our students who viewed him as a symbol of the struggle against racism. It was as if Malcolm X's *endorsement* of reading permitted African American males in particular to feel more comfortable with making mastery of reading and writing part of their identities and less afraid that by taking these pursuits seriously they would be *acting white*.

As students read each text in this first unit, we asked them to add to a chart on which they described how the author or a character might have answered the question why read? Here is one student's "Why Read?" chart.

Why Read? (How Would These People Answer?)

Name	Reasons
Emily Dickinson	*Helps you forget about your problems and makes you feel happy*
Frederick Douglass	*Knowledge is the power for freedom, reading enabled him to free himself and to fight for the freedom of his people*
Malcolm X	*Wanted to be more than others thought of him and to find out the truth*
Claude Brown	*Started getting new ideas about life and enjoyed reading*

Attempting to make the value of reading even more immediate, we also asked students to interview members of their families or communities about what they read and the value they placed on reading. In the process students who had previously connected reading exclusively to school settings began to expand their notions of why people read. In some cases students who thought of themselves as nonreaders or poor readers in the school setting were reminded that they *were* readers in other contexts—such as reading in a church or youth group or reading about sports in the newspaper—that they had never connected with their academic lives. For instance, one young man did not see himself as a reader initially and told us during a literacy history interview that he "didn't enjoy reading that much." But he also told us that he scanned the newspaper for information about sports or about Nicaragua, his birthplace, and that his father often bought him books in Spanish, especially books about Nicaragua.

Reading and Your Goals in Life

I really don't like school a whole lot because I think there really isn't too much need for it. My philosophy is that you should only have to go to school for nine years and then you know everything. Because in life all you need to know how to do is get a job and count your money.

From the beginning of the Academic Literacy course, we had been explicit about *our* goals for students' reading and about why we believed that reading more effectively was so important to students' lives. But despite our arguments, many students were still not making the connection between improving their reading and achieving future success, whether in continued education or training, on the job, or in their personal lives. They spoke as if success would somehow materialize magically when they reached adulthood, irrespective of their reading abilities. During one particularly long class discussion about how students envisioned their futures, one boy kept saying, "I'm just interested in having money, having a nice house and a car." Each time, his fellow students nodded in agreement, failing to see how one's reading ability could either stand in the way of or bring about that appealing vision.

Clearly, we still had some distance to go in helping students find and believe in their own answers to the question, why read? We then asked students to think backward from their hoped-for futures, for example, "money, nice house, car," and to identify how they might get there. As they called out ideas, we listed them on the blackboard in two columns, "long-shot ways" and "slow but steady ways." In the long-shot column we put such answers as becoming a sports superstar, winning the lottery, and getting rich "on the street," that is, through drug sales or other crimes. In the slow-but-steady column we put things like getting a good high school education, passing a test for a city job or a special license, and going on to some kind of higher education, whether college or other training. We then discussed why even though the various slow-but-steady approaches might seem harder they would more likely lead to the futures students wanted.

Building Confidence: Reading Develops on a Continuum

In the collective classroom exploration of the why read question, we also asked students to read about and consider the experiences of unmotivated or struggling readers. One text that struck a responsive chord for many students was an interview with a reluctant fifteen-year-old reader named Kevin Clarke.

> *When I got into the eighth, ninth and tenth grades, reading became a really difficult process because I had to read a lot for school. Each night I might have to read fifteen pages in a biology book, ten pages in an English book, and fifteen more for history. That's an immense amount for me. I start to read, and I get down the first line, OK, second line, OK, third line, OK, but I just can't concentrate after that. I'm reading but my mind is trying to distract me from the book. It's the most frustrating feeling. I say, "OK, think," and slap myself on the face, and go back to the beginning. Or I ask myself, "What have I just read?" and I*

know nothing about what I just read. I might have read six pages and I know nothing.

I get totally uncomfortable when I try to read, and there are always other things I'd rather be doing than making myself uncomfortable and straining myself. I get embarrassed when I read, not because there's someone else around, but because I embarrass myself when I can't do it. I say, "Jeez, you're fifteen and you can't read a whole book, or even a chapter." Why should I put myself in this kind of discomfort on purpose? Sure, I have to do school work, but I can call up a friend to brief me on the chapter, or if I have to answer questions from the reading, I can skim, looking for the important words and write out the answers. I'm definitely smart in a lot of other subjects, but when it gets down to reading, there I am, in the thirteenth percentile.[1]

When students were asked to "write a letter to Kevin" giving him advice about his various reading problems, many wrote about their own feelings of inadequacy as readers along with offering advice that they were just beginning (by late October) to internalize themselves.

Dear Kevin,

I have just read a lot about you and I really understand how you feel about not being able to understand what you're reading. I know how hard and important it is to you, therefore I wrote this letter to give you some suggestions. I want you to get help so you can be a better reader and understand about a certain book you're reading. These suggestions will also help you on how to focus easier.

One of the suggestions I would like to give you is chunking every single paragraph. It's easy. All you have to do is make a slash after each phrase in the sentence. This will break up sentences into pieces small enough for you to understand. Another one is that you should choose your own books. Books that are easy to read and understand. Whatever you're reading, you should read at a comfortable and quiet place which will allow you to read without distraction. And every time you're reading, you should take your time. Don't ever rush. Read slowly so that you can understand every word. I hope you use these great suggestions.

Reading, writing, and talking about the efforts each person in the classroom, including the teacher, had to make to understand various texts—and admitting that such efforts sometimes fail—created the possibility of working together on a problem that many students had previously considered their own private shame.

The following dialogue is another example of an activity that enabled our students to begin to move away from their nonreader identities.

> ## ▐ DIALOGUE BETWEEN A NONREADER AND A READER
>
> ## Materials
>
> The interview from *Speaking of Reading*[2] with a student who only likes reading about serial killers or a different text selection that also describes someone who does not like to read.
>
> ## Procedure
>
> - Set up this situation: the student who only likes books about serial killers and someone such as Malcolm X or other authors from the unit, or even another student who has overcome a struggle with reading, are sitting at a table in a library reading. All of a sudden the fan of serial killer books slams his book down and says, "I hate reading!"
> - Explain to students that they will be writing a two-page dialogue in which the person who now likes to read talks to this student about how to not hate reading so much.
> - Have students read their dialogues aloud with a partner.

As they began to try out the role of more confident reader addressing others who might have reminded many of them of themselves, many students began to make an important shift in their identities as readers. They also began to internalize the notion that, although most people can read certain types of texts quite competently, they may have great difficulty reading other types. With this more nuanced understanding, students moved from seeing reading as an all-or-nothing, succeed-or-fail proposition to seeing reading development as an ongoing process. They began to understand that all readers' abilities vary with the text. With this shift in perspective, students began to feel more hopeful about improving their own reading.

Learning to Choose Books You Like

Interviewer: What kinds of books do you read for SSR?

Student [who had taken Academic Literacy the year before]: I'm trying to find the right stories to read. Last year, my teacher helped me because I was struggling with SSR. I found I liked mysteries or books about criminal activities. It helped me this year because I read Mario Puzo, mobster-type books.

Interviewer: Have you ever read any John Grisham?

Student: No, because I just realized this stuff last year. I heard he was a good writer.

Interviewer: It might be a good summer book.

Student: Or I would also like to try Dean Koontz.

One of our goals in Academic Literacy was to help students begin to think of themselves as readers not just because of what reading could contribute to their future success in the academic and work worlds but because of the pleasure reading could give them. A number of our students who already saw themselves as readers knew where to find books, how to choose books they liked, and who their favorite authors were. But for those who had defined themselves for years as "bored by reading," even the opportunity to choose their own books for pleasure reading presented a problem. Many students have little or no experience reading anything other than what's required for classes. Some told us they had never really liked to read; others recalled that they used to read when they were younger but had stopped in middle school.

We knew that students who had little or no experience of reading for pleasure would be less fluent, motivated, and confident when tackling assigned text than those who had at least enjoyed reading on their own. What these students needed was to hear how their friends, teachers, and other people they knew chose books. They needed to become familiar with popular authors and with the different types of books that might appeal to them. In the first weeks of the course, we spent time talking about where to find books and how to choose among them, and we asked students to keep a list of different ways to choose books, as in this example:

> ***How to Choose a Book***
>
> *Read the back of the book to see if it is interesting.*
>
> *Find the subject I like to read.*
>
> *Ask a friend.*
>
> *Look for an author you like.*
>
> *Skim through the book—read a few pages.*
>
> *Find a book that relates to you.*

Giving Books the Ten-Page Chance

We also spent time discussing what to do when you find that the book you chose isn't as interesting as you had expected. We explained that adults do not necessarily finish every book they start. With so many wonderful books to choose from for pleasure reading, why would anyone spend time on a book he or she didn't like? We proposed that students give a chosen book a *ten-page chance:* "If the book captures your interest by the time you've read the first ten pages, keep reading. But if after ten pages you still don't like the book, stop and find another one, either on your own or with the help of a friend, parent or teacher. Finally, if at the end of ten pages you aren't sure what to think of the book, consider giving it another ten-page chance, after which you can decide what to do."

The crucial point for students to understand is that when it comes to pleasure reading, they can choose what to read and what not to read. Abandoning a book in that context isn't the sign of a poor reader but of an intelligent, discriminating reader who knows what he or she wants from reading. Good readers give a text a chance, but if it doesn't meet their interest or their needs, they trade it in for something that will.

Silent Sustained Reading: Making Time for Reading

First Student: I wouldn't read books if she didn't make us.

Interviewer: Why is that?

First Student: It's fun, but if you ain't got to do it, then what's the use of doing it?

Second Student: It's not an everyday thing.

Recognizing what you like to read is a first step toward becoming an experienced and, eventually, a lifelong reader. But having the time and encouragement to read is just as important, especially for students not in the habit of reading. Twice a week, we set aside twenty minutes of class time for students to do silent sustained reading (SSR). Here is how we set it up (the SSR log this activity mentions is described later).

SETTING UP SILENT SUSTAINED READING (SSR)

Procedure

- Explain that SSR will be a regular routine throughout the class.
- Explain the reasons for doing SSR: to gain fluency, engagement, agency.
- Explain the requirements for an SSR book to students:
  It must be a book (no magazines, newspapers, or comic books).
  It must have more words than pictures.
  It must be something you are interested in.
  It must be something your parents, if asked, would allow you to read.
  It must not be a book you are reading for another class.
- Explain the SSR ground rules to students:
  If you leave your book at home, choose another one off the shelf for the day.
  Stay in your seat so others aren't distracted.
  Do not do homework.
  Do not talk.
  Do your best to read for the whole time.
  Write in your SSR log when we finish.
  Read at least two hundred pages per month, preferably in the same book.

As students began preparing to choose their books, we took them on several trips to the local library as well as to the school library. We found that many self-identified nonreaders needed our assistance and encouragement in finding books that would capture their interest and be within their comfort level as readers.

Finally, in setting up SSR as an essential course component, we knew that well-stocked classroom libraries would be critical to building students' engagement and fluency. The most important feature of a good classroom library is that it have enough variety in topics, genres, and reading levels to appeal to the full range of classroom readers. We knew it was important to include both fiction and nonfiction, like biographies, historical narratives, and informational texts about topics of interest to youths. We became, as many of our teacher colleagues have learned to be, expert scroungers. We frequented used book stores, flea markets, and thrift shops and held a book drive in which parents, students, and other teachers solicited used books from their neighborhoods and local businesses.

Avoiding Common SSR Pitfalls

Interviewer: Why do you think you started to like reading?

Student: At first I just pretended to be reading, but then one day I really started reading. [The teacher] started getting on my case. Ever since then, I have been reading.

Like any classroom practice, SSR requires certain conditions for success. Teachers must be convinced of its value. They should be knowledgeable about helping students identify good reading choices. Students need easy access to a wide variety of popular fiction and nonfiction. Teachers would be wise to set up an accountability system that encourages students to complete books and receive course credit. And finally, students must be encouraged to share books with one another—both books that they have liked and books they did not like but think someone else might.

We know from observation and from our own experience that when these conditions are not met, SSR can be a dispiriting waste of time for everyone. Students can end up pretending to read or using SSR time to sleep, whisper or pass notes to each other, or disrupt others' reading. Teachers can end up serving as reading police, constantly patrolling the room to try to force compliance, or they may just give up and pretend to believe that everyone is reading.

In our Academic Literacy version of SSR, students were required to finish at least one two-hundred-page book (or a minimum of two hundred pages from a longer book) by the end of each six-week marking period. Readers monitored their progress during class sessions in an SSR log. But they were also expected to take their books home and continue reading there, simply being sure to bring the book to class for each SSR session. In order to complete a book and get credit for it during the marking period, students had to read at home. We introduced SSR with clear expectations for student accountability so that the strategy of pretending to read would not work in Academic Literacy.

Developing the Internal Metacognitive Conversation with SSR Logs

> *They teach you to think about what you think about when you read. Like when we do SSR, and we have to write in our log after, it's not like, "Write about what happened in the book," it's like, "Were you looking out the window? How much of the time you were supposed to be reading were you concentrating?"*

A very important variation we brought to our Academic Literacy version of SSR was to ask students to focus in their logs on how they were reading rather than on a book's content. Because we had spent a good deal of time developing an external conversation about metacognition in our classrooms and had given students many opportunities to see us think aloud as we read through texts cold—they now had some preparation for focusing on their own internal metacognitive conversation. We asked students to think of themselves as scientists whose research subject was themselves. They would observe themselves reading and then take notes on their reading process.

At the end of each SSR session, we had students write for five minutes about how they had gone about reading during that session. We urged them to copy the sentence starters below into their logs as prompts for this reflective writing. This activity served two purposes. It gave students practice in reflecting on their own reading processes, helping them become more aware of what they did and did not do as they read. It also allowed us to learn about the problems they encountered and the solutions they came up with as they read.

As part of our effort to build accountability into SSR, we also asked students to write a two-part reflective letter to their teacher each time they finished reading a book, as described in the following student instructions.

SSR LOGS (METACOGNITIVE LOGS)

Materials

Loose-leaf-binder paper (cut in half crosswise) for inside pages, colored paper (cut in half crosswise) for covers.

Procedure

- Make the logs: stack ten pieces of binder paper and a cover, fold the stack in half, and staple it in the middle (this can be done beforehand by volunteers or by a classroom assembly line).
- On the inside cover, have students enter the following *sentence starters,* designed to help them get started writing about their reading process:

  While I was reading

  > I got confused when . . .
  >
  > I was distracted by . . .
  >
  > I started to think about . . .
  >
  > I got stuck when . . .
  >
  > The time went quickly because . . .
  >
  > A word/some words I didn't know were . . .
  >
  > I stopped because . . .
  >
  > I lost track of everything except . . .
  >
  > I figured out that . . .
  >
  > I first thought . . . but then I realized . . .

- Ask students to record the following at the top of each page:

  Date   Book   Title   Page # Started   Page # Ended   Time Spent Reading

- After each SSR session, have students fill out their logs using the heading and one or more of the sentence starters.
- When students are finished, you may want to collect the logs and keep them in the classroom (so you can look at them, and so students don't lose them).
- On the inside back cover of the log, you may want to have students make the following status chart to help you track your students' reading progress at a glance. For the status category on the chart, create three symbols that indicate (1) the student has finished the book, (2) the student started the book but doesn't intend to finish it, and (3) the student has started the book and is still reading it.

  Date   Book   Title   Pg # Started, Ended   Status

- Have students make entries on the chart at the end of each month and whenever they finish or change books. (We began using the chart on the inside back cover because we found students had a tendency to lose the logs when they took them home, probably because the logs are relatively small. So we now have students use the main log only for reading done in class, but we track all the pages they read in each book, whether at home or at school, through this chart.

SSR BOOK: MONTHLY ASSIGNMENT

Instructions

You will be sharing your SSR book in two ways. The first way is by writing a letter to your Academic Literacy teacher about the book and what you have learned about yourself as a reader by reading this book. The second way is by creating a book poster in which you choose quotes from the book to illustrate.

1. The Letter

Write a letter to your Academic Literacy teacher. This letter should be at least one page long and include the following information:

About the book. Give the title, author, and a brief summary of the book's plot. Choose one character that you liked or disliked most in the book. Describe this character, and explain why you felt the way you did about this character. How did this book compare to other books you have read so far this term? Would you recommend this book to a friend? Why or why not?

About yourself as a reader. What, if anything, are you noticing about yourself as a reader that is different from the way you read at the beginning of the term? Are your interests, skills, or habits changing in any way? What, if anything, is surprising you? Did you meet any of the reading goals that you set for yourself last month (to read faster, not wait until the last minute, try longer or different types of books, and so on)? What are your reading goals for this coming month?

2. The Book Poster

Choose six quotations (usually a sentence or two) from your book that you found interesting. Divide a large sheet of paper into six sections, and copy one quotation onto the bottom of each section. Then illustrate each quotation, either symbolically or literally. You may draw or use magazine or newspaper pictures or computer graphics. Be prepared to explain your choice of quotations and illustrations.

Sharing Books and Book Talk

One important element of the social aspect we built into our SSR routines was the regular time in which students *very briefly* checked in with the class about the books they were reading. This helped maintain accountability and also gave listening students ideas about books they might want to read.

Although it took longer than we had expected, by the middle of the first semester of Academic Literacy, we were convinced that all but two or three students in each of our twelve classes were actually reading and finishing self-selected books, with some of them reading as many as one a month. With a few exceptions, students, either on their own or with our help, were able to find books that were interesting and accessible. For English as a second language learners and mainstreamed special education students we used high-interest, low-reading-level books. For most students the pressure of knowing that within a six-week marking period

---

Procedure

- At some point in the first week or two of each month, go around the room and have students report on their reading situation.
- Have each student show the class what book he or she is reading and tell the class one of the following:

  I'm reading this book.

  I'm giving this book a(nother) ten-page chance.

  I don't like this book; I'm going to choose another one.

  Students who have not yet settled into a book will likely get a hint that they need to find something quickly, because most of their classmates are already in the middle of a book!

---

they had to finish a book and do a public sharing of it with the rest of the class through monthly SSR projects seemed to speed up their decision-making process. They chose books quickly and as a result began to learn more about what they liked and didn't like for recreational reading.

We noticed as the weeks went by that students were passing books around to each other and trying out new authors. In one class a group of Chinese American boys had spent the first few months of SSR exclusively reading Dungeons and Dragons–type fantasies. By spring, however, they had all read April Sinclair's *Coffee Will Make You Black,* a book that had initially circulated primarily among the African American and Latino students. Another student spent the entire first semester reading mysteries by R. L. Stine (the all-time favorite author of our students, according to our end-of-year reading survey). By spring semester this student had started to read V. C. Andrews, and she ended the year with a Stephen King book that she planned to finish over the summer.

Building Concentration, Stamina, and Fluency

Even when our students found books that were interesting, they often found it difficult to read for twenty minutes at a time. In fact many lacked the mental stamina to read for more than a few minutes before their attention wandered. To build their stamina, we began the SSR sessions with ten minutes of reading, only gradually working up to twenty minutes or more. By the end of the year, some students actually asked if we could extend the SSR time or have it more often. In one class the students lobbied for an entire block (one hundred minutes) of SSR time and stayed engaged in their reading for the whole time!

The history book is really boring. But [the Academic Literacy course] helped me pace myself, even if it is boring. Even if you don't want to read, you can.

In addition to developing students' sense of what they liked to read and building up their stamina, and in turn their fluency, we worked on helping students increase their ability not only to notice and describe but also to control their reading processes. First, we gave students explicit strategies for controlling their concentration, helping them become more aware of what distracted them and of the conditions under which they read most effectively.

What Channel Is Your Mind On?

We read excerpts from *Keeping a Head in School,* a book about how the brain works that is written for young people and focuses on attention and concentration.[3] In describing attention, the author compares the different places students' attention might be focused to television channels. As one student described it, "In Academic Literacy they taught you about different channels of your brain. Like my teacher would say, 'You have one channel for being with your friends, and one channel for getting dressed, and you have a channel for being in school.' And so we would be supposed to ask ourselves, 'What channel am I on? Am I on my school channel?'"

We also spent a good bit of time reading and discussing the Concentration Cockpit (Figure 4.1), talking about the different kinds of control students wanted to develop. After this discussion we asked each student to write a letter to the teacher describing his or her own strengths and weaknesses in paying attention while reading.

I think there are certain things that will allow people to pay attention more. For example last week I was in my class and I hadn't combed my hair yet. So I wasn't focused on our classroom work I was too busy thinking about combing my hair. Then I finally went to the bathroom and combed my hair. When I was through I came back to class and I was able to focus and pay attention.

As students began tuning in to how well they did or didn't pay attention while reading and to the circumstances likely to distract them, they often recognized reading behaviors they were not controlling but could potentially control. After introducing various strategies for paying attention, we asked them to develop a plan for regaining lost focus while reading (see the following example).

FIGURE 4.1

Attention: Keeping the Body and Mind in Control

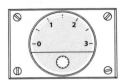

MOOD CONTROL: Not Getting Much Too Sad or Much Too Happy at the Wrong Times

The Concentration Cockpit

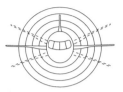

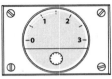

SENSORY FILTRATION CONTROL: Not Paying Attention to Unimportant Sounds and Sights

MOTOR/VERBAL CONTROL: Not Wasting Movement and Talking

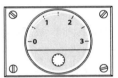

SOCIAL CONTROL: Tuning Out Other Kids When You Need To

APPETITE CONTROL: Not Always Wanting Things and Looking Ahead

BEHAVIORAL CONTROL: Thinking Before You Do Things

FREE FLIGHT CONTROL: Not Daydreaming

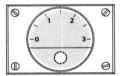

MEMORY CONTROL: Remembering Important Things

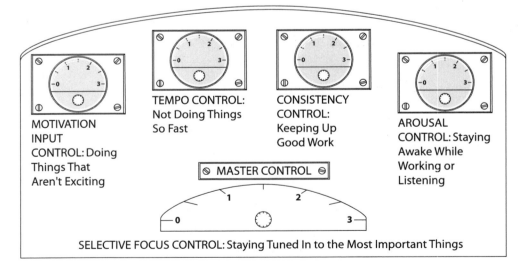

MOTIVATION INPUT CONTROL: Doing Things That Aren't Exciting

TEMPO CONTROL: Not Doing Things So Fast

CONSISTENCY CONTROL: Keeping Up Good Work

AROUSAL CONTROL: Staying Awake While Working or Listening

MASTER CONTROL

SELECTIVE FOCUS CONTROL: Staying Tuned In to the Most Important Things

0 = no control; 1 = poor control; 2 = good control; 3 = excellent control.

Source: *M. Levine,* Keeping a Head in School: A Student's Book About Learning Abilities and Learning Disorders *(Cambridge, Mass.: Educators' Publishing Services, 1990), p. 41.*

My Plan for Distractions

Distraction #1	*Daydream about many things like about a person or place or thing*
What I can do	*Stop myself and train my mind how not to wander*
Distraction #2	*Things I may want like getting my watch fixed or the shoes I want, and so on*
What I can do	*Tell myself to stop things like that from running through my head and write them down if they're important enough*

Throughout the year, we reminded students to look back at these goals and plans. Over time they began taking more responsibility for their mental behavior, many becoming more attentive not just during SSR but during class in general. This focus on increasing their mental control seemed to transfer to other classes as well and to increase their sense of agency, their feeling of being proactive rather than passive participants in their own lives.

Building Beyond the Social and Personal Foundation

Throughout the year, we continued to reinforce and further develop the personal and social dimensions of reading apprenticeship. Academic Literacy students continued to explore their personal reading preferences and habits and to talk with teachers and other students about their reading processes, problems, and solutions. But though we knew that the social and personal dimensions of reading apprenticeship were the necessary motivational base for Academic Literacy, we also knew that they were not a sufficient foundation on which to develop our students' success as readers of academic texts. In the next chapter we discuss the mental toolbelt our students began to develop as the Academic Literacy course continued.

Notes

1. Quoted in N. Rosenthal, *Speaking of Reading* (Portsmouth, N.H.: Heinemann, 1995).

2. Rosenthal, *Speaking of Reading.*

3. M. Levine, *Keeping a Head in School: A Student's Book About Learning Abilities and Learning Disorders* (Cambridge, Mass.: Educators' Publishing Services, 1990).

Chapter 5

Acquiring Cognitive Tools for Reading

IN TALKING WITH our Academic Literacy students about reading for understanding, reading with your mind as opposed to just reading with your mouth, we had often used the idea of reading as problem solving. Being able to monitor and control their attention while reading and to be specific about problems in understanding texts were important starting points for our students as they began to believe they could actually increase their ability to read with understanding. But without a repertoire of specific cognitive strategies and the ability to use these strategies, they were unlikely to solve the variety of reading comprehension problems they would likely encounter in academic texts. And without some degree of success with academic texts, even the most engaged readers could become discouraged and once again disengaged. Clearly, if students were willing to struggle with challenging texts, we would need to equip them with the appropriate problem-solving tools. This chapter examines a variety of those tools and two methods in particular that we use for teaching them: thinking aloud and reciprocal teaching.

Teaching Students Strategies for Problem Solving

Our students knew from their own life experiences that whether one is fixing a car or getting through the hardest level of a video game, solving different problems calls for different sets of tools and strategies and the ability to use them appropriately. Sometime toward the middle of the first unit, we reminded students that understanding difficult texts is also a form of problem solving—one to which they could apply a variety of cognitive tools. We said we would help them assemble a *mental toolbelt* for reading, with at least four key comprehension tools: questioning, summarizing, predicting, and clarifying. We suggested they record in their unit learning logs two statements: "In this class I will learn about reading strategies—what to do when I get stuck," and, "In this class I will put together my own mental toolbelt to help me fix reading comprehension problems."

Helping Students Become Strategic Readers

When I read now—we learned about this thing called metacognition: when you read, you think about reading while you are reading 'cause if you don't think about reading while you are reading, your mind will drift off—I think about the purpose of why I am reading something. If you told me to read something and tell you something about it when I am done, I would read it in a certain way. If you just told me to take notes on this, then I would read a different way.

In talking about the mental toolbelt we explained that all the tools students would learn to use were intended to help them better understand difficult texts. We taught them about a number of different comprehension strategies, or tools, and some common uses for each. Some students used several tools on a regular basis, and other students used two or three tools most consistently. Our goal in teaching them to use different tools was to make them strategic readers, so that when they had a comprehension problem they could choose an appropriate tool and work to solve the problem independently. The choice of tool or cognitive strategy would depend on the nature of this problem, the student's purpose for reading, and the student's comfort level with each of the tools. In short, students would have a variety of tools to draw on when they started to sense they were no longer making meaning of a text.

Teaching Strategies in Context

The aim of all Academic Literacy work is to help students become increasingly independent readers. To that end it is crucial that students become adept, comfortable, and independent in using the comprehension strategies in their mental toolbelts. We knew we couldn't just teach a comprehension strategy and expect students to use it. Knowing that full acquisition of strategies develops only with practice over time, we first introduced new cognitive strategies with less demanding texts. However, we always chose texts that were thematically related to the units. For example, during the Reading Self and Society unit, students practiced summarizing with an excerpt from *Woman Warrior,* which explores issues of language and literacy learning in an American public school from the point of view of a young Chinese immigrant. We kept the excerpt short and had students work in groups to practice summarizing different parts of the text. Through repeated cycles of guided individual and group practice, students gained the facility to use each new strategy with increasingly challenging texts. Ultimately, they practiced with the kinds of texts they were expected to read and understand in their various subject-area classes.

Individual and Group Responsibility for Learning

As our students practiced and began to incorporate new cognitive strategies for understanding texts, we asked them to evaluate how particular strategies were working for them in their problem-solving efforts. Students were asked to share with the class what they did to create a summary, how they figured out whether they needed to clarify something in the text, how they composed a question, and ultimately, what difference these strategies made for their comprehension of class texts. In this process, individual students became more aware of the specific strategies that worked for them. This tied into their developing a more detailed picture of themselves as readers, coming to know in some detail what is useful for them as readers.

Students also came to view one another as resources for learning to use strategies successfully. Because the Academic Literacy course was at heart a collaborative inquiry into reading, students did much of their work in groups. But throughout the course we made it clear that being collaborative meant *partners* coming together, each with his or her own contribution. In other words, students could not simply sit back and wait for the more competent or engaged readers to do their work for them. We talked with our students about gatekeeper texts that determine their future education and career options, such as the texts found in standardized assessments from state-mandated reading tests to nationally administered SAT and ACT exams. We talked about the fact that in terms of many of these high-stakes situations, students can only make use of those cognitive strategies they have individually mastered. Keenly aware of this reality, we used a combination of group and individual activities, doing what we could to make sure each student learned and had many opportunities to practice using these cognitive strategies.

Modeling Problem Solving

As we had done when we used think-alouds to give students the idea of the metacognitive processes involved in reading, we sometimes modeled various comprehension strategies using think-alouds, working with texts we had not read beforehand, like that morning's newspaper editorial or a current magazine article. Using a teacher think-aloud to model cognitive strategies helped remind students how complex the meaning-making process underlying these strategies really is. How do readers decide what is important to include or to leave out when summarizing an article? What exactly is it about the language or structure of a particular text that helps readers pick up and follow the strands of an argument as they attempt to predict an author's mental moves in an editorial? Once students have seen teachers model strategies, making them visible through the think-aloud process, they can begin to practice thinking aloud strategically themselves.

The following lesson plan describes the steps in this modeling process. It focuses on teaching the comprehension strategy of predicting plus a few additional comprehension strategies that we have found especially useful.[1]

TEACHING THE THINK-ALOUD PROCESS

Purpose

The think-aloud process helps students practice the mental activities, or strategies, engaged in by good readers. It helps them focus on comprehension, and it helps the teacher know when and how students' comprehension goes awry.

Initial Procedure

• Demonstrate the process of using the following types of think-aloud statements while reading a passage you have not seen before to the class.

Types of Think-Alouds

Predicting

I predict . . .

In the next part I think . . .

I think this is . . .

Picturing

I picture . . .

I can see . . .

Making connections

This is like a . . .

This reminds me of . . .

(Continued)

TEACHING THE THINK-ALOUD PROCESS (cont.)

    Identifying a problem
      I got confused when . . .
      I'm not sure of . . .
      I didn't expect . . .
    Using fix-ups
      I think I'll have to [reread, or take some other action to help comprehension]
      Maybe I'll need to [read on, or persevere in some other way]

- After a few demonstrations, ask students to use a checklist to identify your think-alouds.
    Think-Aloud Checklist
      Make a tally mark each time you hear one of the following:
        Predicting
        Picturing
        Making connections
        Identifying problems
        Using fix-ups
        Other

- Go over the checklists with the class.

Scaffolded Practice Procedure

- *Paired reading.* After students have a few opportunities to listen to your modeling of think-alouds and to identify them using the checklist, have students practice think-alouds with a partner. Each student should read a passage, pausing to make think-aloud statements as his or her partner listens. You may want to ask listeners to use the checklist, tallying the think-alouds for the reader.
- *Thinking silently.* After they have several opportunities to work with partners, ask students to practice reading independently, paying attention to their thoughts as they read and using the checklist to tally the different types of thinking silently, or strategies, they engage in.
- *Ongoing assessment.* Give students time, especially at first, to share their self-assessments. Have a class discussion on what is hard about trying to think aloud as one reads. Ask students how they went about trying to solve any problems they had. Finally, ask them to reflect on how using think-alouds is affecting them as readers.

Applications of Practice Procedure

Choose your applications depending on your purpose.

- Have students keep a reading folder in which they enter the tallies of their thoughts at various points in the school year. During grading periods, students can assess their growth as readers, noting any change in the kinds of thinking they do as they read.
- Guide students in discussing the meaning of texts that they have read in pairs or independently using thinking aloud or thinking silently. This is particularly useful with texts such as primary source documents, scientific reports, essays, and difficult literature, which give readers opportunities to make interpretations, draw implications, and link text concepts to other classroom activities.
- Use the think-aloud procedure to demonstrate the different ways proficient readers approach different kinds of texts for different purposes.

The point of having students practice to the degree described in this lesson plan is to ultimately enable them to use the strategies automatically and effortlessly—just as an automobile driver moves from student driver to fully licensed driver once he or she can fairly automatically manage the clutch and the gas pedal, check the rearview mirrors, monitor traffic and road conditions, and steer accurately all at the same time.

Once students have had a significant amount of practice deliberately using various strategies, they begin to internalize them and to use them unconsciously. In a sense, then, the aim in teaching cognitive strategies is the opposite of making the invisible visible. Teachers as master readers make their own normally invisible reading processes visible to their student apprentices. They then turn around and help students learn and practice the strategies until these tools start to become second nature, eventually becoming a part of students' unconscious reading process—in other words, once again invisible.

Assembling the Mental Toolbelt

Embedding cognitive strategies practice in texts linked to the themes we were exploring and in the central habit of thinking aloud was crucial to our design of explicit instruction in comprehension. In addition, a process called reciprocal teaching (RT), developed by cognitive researchers Annemarie Palinscar and Ann Brown,[2] provided an important point of reference for our work in developing the cognitive dimension in our classrooms. RT is a process that helps students monitor their reading comprehension and practice and internalize four cognitive strategies known to be key parts of the repertoire of proficient readers: *questioning, summarizing, predicting,* and *clarifying.*

In RT, teachers and students participate in a structured dialogue about a text, using these four comprehension strategies. The teacher and students take turns as the *discussion leader,* directing the dialogue and leading the group through the strategies. Over time and with practice the individual students become increasingly able to assess their own understanding of a text and increasingly adept at using the strategies to aid comprehension. Designed originally for a small group in a remedial setting, RT has been adapted to whole-class teaching and to peer-led small-group work in classrooms.

RT is an important reference point for our work because it shares important features with our reading apprenticeship approach. Most important, in the RT model, reading is understood as a problem-solving activity requiring the reader's mental engagement and awareness of his or her reading process. Readers become metacognitive, monitoring and checking their comprehension. Second, RT makes the invisible visible by explicitly teaching students to carry out the critical cognitive strategies proficient readers use for problem solving. Third, students practice these strategies with the aim of internalizing them over time. Fourth, students have access to the help of their teacher and peers. They can draw on the resources of the group to solve their own comprehension problems, and they can also see how other readers use comprehension strategies to make sense of texts. Finally, in the RT process, students learn and practice cognitive strategies in the context of purposeful reading rather than practicing these strategies as decontextualized reading skills.

We saw reciprocal teaching as a way to help students internalize the most important strategies competent readers use to gauge their comprehension, not as a process our students would necessarily use in its entirety very often. First we introduced and practiced various types of questioning for several weeks with different texts and types of individual and group activities so that our students could gain confidence deliberately using strategies to support reading comprehension with a limited number of tools. Then we moved on to teach summarizing, clarifying, and predicting. Once they had had practice using all four strategies, we could move on to reciprocal teaching itself.

The remainder of this chapter outlines the ideas and activities we used to teach these four strategies; discusses the technique of chunking texts, which makes it easier for students to apply comprehension strategies; and shows how our students used the reciprocal teaching process to develop proficiency in applying their new skills.

Questioning

One of the most powerful cognitive tools for reading comprehension is questioning. We used two questioning activities in Academic Literacy, with the aim of getting students to engage more actively with texts. Framing questions about a text pushes students to read with greater purpose and therefore with greater focus. Unfortunately, the idea of asking questions in class evokes negative associations for many students. We told our students that in this class, and especially with this particular cognitive strategy, asking a question would show what they knew, not what they didn't know.

In both of the following activities, students compose questions about the text they are reading. The twist is that they must know the answers to these questions from their reading of the story or article at hand. They then get credit for their questions.

The first activity is based on a procedure called ReQuest.[3]

REQUEST

Procedure

- Have students write questions based on their reading of a particular text. The reading and writing may be done in class or as homework.
- Ask a student volunteer to read one of his or her questions to the group.
- Ask students to raise their hands if they can answer the question.
- Have the first student call on one of these volunteers to answer the question.
- After the volunteer answers the question, have this student ask the class one of his or her questions.
- Continue the process until everyone in the class has asked and answered one question. To ensure everyone's participation, no one can answer a second question until everyone has answered one.

For example, after our students read a section of Frederick Douglass's autobiography in class, we asked each student to write five questions based on that text that he or she could answer. We told the students that they should think of themselves as teachers, identifying the questions they would expect their students to be able to answer if they had read and understood the text. We also told them it did not matter how simple or difficult their own questions were so long as they knew the answers to them. We then went around the room using the ReQuest procedure, continuing until each student had both asked and answered a question.

ReQuest became a routine classroom activity, with the question writing becoming a frequent homework assignment. During the ten minutes or so that it took to run through this activity on a given text, the process invariably revealed both what students understood and what they misunderstood. When someone's answer was not acceptable to the student who wrote the question, a class discussion would usually settle the disagreement.

As students became familiar and comfortable with the ReQuest process, we used Taffy Raphael's work on Question-Answer Relationships[4] (QARs) to create other comprehension strategy activities. Raphael discusses four types of questions: *right there, pulling it together, author and me,* and *on my own.* The questions require different types of interaction with the text.

Because we found that although our students typically understood the *right there* and *pulling it together* questions easily, they often had trouble with the *author and me* and *on my own* questions, we used a variety of simple texts in the beginning. In addition, we talked with students about why some questions are harder to create than others. Here is an example of one simple text we made up, followed by a definition and examples of each kind of question.

> *David woke up fifteen minutes late. As soon as he saw the clock, he jumped out of bed and headed for the shower, afraid he'd miss the bus again. He looked in the dryer for his favorite jeans, but they were actually still in the washing machine. "Dang! I told my sister to put my stuff in the dryer! Now what am I gonna wear today?" After settling for a pair of baggy shorts and a Hilfiger rugby shirt, he grabbed a bag of chips and a soda from the kitchen, and searched frantically for his history book. When he found it, he put it in his backpack, along with his break-fast, his hat, and his lucky deck of cards. As he ran to the bus stop, he told himself, "I will not stay up late watching wrestling anymore!"*

A right there question is a question whose answer is right in the text—all the reader has to do is copy it down or repeat it. A right there question about the paragraph in the example might be, "What did David do as soon as he saw the clock?" or "What did he tell himself as he ran to the bus stop?"

A pulling it together question is a question whose answer is in the text, but the reader has to pull it together from different parts of the text—he or she cannot simply copy from one place. A pulling it together question about the example might be, "How did David get ready to leave the house?" or, "What did David look for before he left the house?"

An author and me question is a question whose answer is not in the text. The reader has to use the information provided in the text *and* his or her own schema to figure out the answer. In other words, the author provides information that can help answer the question but does not provide the answer itself. An author and me question about the example might be, "Where was David heading that morning?" or, "What time of day was David getting ready to go?"

An on my own question is a question whose answer is not in the text. The reader does not have to have read the text to answer the question, but reading the text will inform his or her answer. An on my own question about the example might be, "Should teenagers be able to watch television on school nights?" or "Should parents always wake their kids up in the morning?"

In our discussions we divided these four types of questions into two groups. Right there and pulling it together questions we characterized as *in the text* questions—questions whose answers can be found somewhere in the text and thus are relatively easy to answer. There is often only one right answer to in the text questions. Author and me and on my own questions we characterized as *in my mind* questions. Because their answers cannot be found in the text and because they may have more than one right answer, these questions are more difficult. Right there and pulling it together questions tend to appear on things like reading quizzes, whereas on my own questions tend to come up during class discussions and author and me questions tend to be used in essay assignments.

The following activity, which we call Question Around, is a relatively quick activity we did a few times after we introduced the different question types. It is very similar to the ReQuest activity, and it serves two purposes: it gives students practice with the different types of questions, and it helps them review the previous night's reading. We found it important to again set the rule that no one may answer a second question until everyone in the class has answered one. This prevents the more enthusiastic students from dominating the activity and ensures that all students participate eventually. It also lets the teacher know whether some students are struggling with the question types and need help from the teacher and other students.

QUESTION AROUND

Procedure

- For homework the previous night, have students generate a number of questions about the text they read.
- In class, have a student read one of his or her questions.
- Ask students to raise their hands if they know the answer to the question *and* the type of question it is.
- Have the student who posed the question call on someone who raised his or her hand.
- Have that student answer the question and tell the class which type of question it is.
- Have that student read one of his or her questions to the class.
- Repeat the process until everyone in the class has asked at least one question.

The following activity is an example of the way we continued to use the social dimension of the classroom to reinforce students' understanding. Because students in each group in this activity have to come to consensus about which questions fit where, they have some good discussions about what makes a particular question fit better into one category than another.

CATEGORIZING QUESTIONS

Materials

A text that students will read and generate questions about, poster paper, and colored markers.

Procedure

- Have students individually generate two or three questions of each type about the previous night's reading.
- In class the next day, ask students to get in groups and share their questions with each other.
- Ask each group of students to create four posters: one for each type of question. On each poster, students must write four questions of that type.
- Once students agree that all the questions are correctly categorized, ask everyone in the group to sign each poster to signal their agreement.
- Display all the posters, and ask students to go around the room looking at other groups' posters.
- Ask students who find a question they think is incorrectly categorized to put a star next to it.
- Once all the students have seen all the posters, guide the class in analyzing each of the starred questions in order to decide where it belongs.

After using several easy texts to introduce students to the four types of questions, we began to have our students work with these questions in their reading of more difficult texts in the Reading Self and Society unit. Several of us had students first practice this with the following excerpt from Frederick Douglass's autobiography.

> My mistress was, as I have said, a kind and tender-hearted woman; and in the simplicity of her soul commenced, when I first went to live with her, to treat me as she supposed one human being ought to treat another. In entering upon the duties of a slaveholder, she did not seem to perceive that I sustained to her the relation of a mere chattel, and that for her to treat me as a human being was not only wrong, but dangerously so. Slavery proved as injurious to her as it did to me. When I went there, she was a pious, warm, and tender-hearted woman. There was no sorrow or suffering for which she had not a tear. She had bread for the hungry, clothes for the naked, and comfort for every mourner that came within her reach. Slavery soon proved its ability to divest her of these heavenly qualities. Under its influence, the tender heart became stone, and the lamblike disposition gave way to one of tiger-like fierceness. The first step in her downward course was in her ceasing to instruct me. She now commenced to practice her husband's precepts. She finally became even more violent in her opposition than

her husband himself. She was not satisfied with simply doing as well as he had commanded; she seemed anxious to do better. Nothing seemed to make her more angry than to see me with a newspaper. She seemed to think that here lay the danger. I have had her rush at me with a face made all up of fury, and snatch from me a newspaper, in a manner that fully revealed her apprehension. She was an apt woman; and a little experience soon demonstrated, to her satisfaction, that education and slavery were incompatible with each other.

From this time I was most narrowly watched. If I was in a separate room any considerable length of time, I was sure to be suspected of having a book, and was at once called to give an account of myself. All this, however, was too late. The first step had been taken. Mistress, in teaching me the alphabet, had given me the inch, and no precaution could prevent me from taking the all.

The plan which I adopted, and the one by which I was most successful, was that of making friends of all the little white boys whom I met in the street. As many of these as I could, I converted into teachers. With their kindly aid, obtained at different times and in different places, I finally succeeded in learning to read. When I was sent on errands, I always took my book with me, and by going one part of my errand quickly, I found time to get a lesson before my return. I used also to carry bread with me, enough of which was always in the house, and to which I was always welcome; for I was much better off in this regard than many of the poor white children in our neighborhood. This bread I used to bestow upon the hungry little urchins, who, in return, would give me that more valuable bread of knowledge. I am strongly tempted to give the names of two or three of those little boys, as a testimonial of the gratitude and affection I bear them. But prudence forbids;—not that it would injure me, but it might embarrass them; for it is almost an unpardonable offence to teach slaves to read in this Christian country. It is enough to say of the dear little fellows, that they lived on Philpot Street, very near Durgin and Bailey's ship-yard. I used to talk this matter of slavery over with them. I would sometimes say to them, I wished I could be as free as they would be when they got to be men. "You will be free as soon as you are twenty-one, but I am a slave for life! Have not I as good a right to be free as you have?" These words used to trouble them; they would express for me the liveliest sympathy, and console me with the hope that something would occur by which I might be free.[5]

Here are some of the questions students wrote after reading this excerpt.

Right There Questions

Who taught Frederick Douglass the alphabet?

What did he use the bread for?

Pulling It Together Question

What did Frederick Douglass do when his mistress stopped teaching him how to read?

Text and Me Question

How did Frederick Douglass's mistress change over time?

On My Own Question

Why would one group of people try to prevent another group from learning to read?

Throughout the Academic Literacy course, and particularly during the first several months, we returned to homework and in-class activities that reinforced students' understanding of these four types of questions in a variety of ways. For instance, one activity we came back to was categorizing questions (described earlier), because defending their categorization of a question or arguing that a classmate's question actually belonged in another category sent students back to the text again and again.

To help students better understand text and me questions we did a minilesson using a Venn diagram to illustrate the difference between information that can be found stated in the text itself and information that the reader brings to the text or deduces from the text to help make sense of it. For example, a text and me question about the excerpt from Frederick Douglass's autobiography would be, How old was Frederick Douglass when he died? Although the answer in that form is not in the text, the introduction to Douglass's essay contained in the anthology we used states that Douglass lived from 1817 to 1895, and therefore the information needed to answer the question *is* in the text. When students use their background knowledge of addition and subtraction, they can easily figure out that Douglass was seventy-eight when he died. This approach helped some students better understand the concept of text and me questions, but throughout the course we returned again and again to the relationship between reader knowledge and text content.

Summarizing

In our work with Academic Literacy students, we came to believe that summarizing is one of the most frequently assigned but rarely (explicitly) taught comprehension strategies students are expected to master. From upper primary grades on, students are asked to write summaries of textbook chapters, novels, science lab findings, and written materials of all kinds. Yet when we asked students about their experience with summarizing, we discovered that they had little real understanding of how to summarize effectively. Students wrote about copying summaries from the jackets of novels or picking out random parts of a textbook chapter to copy as a summary. Although they knew that a summary involved pulling together the most important parts of a text and writing them down in a shortened form, most had little idea about how to decide what was important or how to put key ideas into their own words. Some students noted that they had trouble knowing how much information to put in a summary to capture the main idea. Others found they had the opposite problem. One student wrote, "Summarizing is hard for me because I can't pull out the main subject. I always get into detail." Still others had difficulty deciding what the main ideas of the text were and what the details were.

During the Reading Self and Society unit, we had students summarize paragraphs from various articles we were reading. We started by having them read an article about the importance of an extensive vocabulary for success in the business world. We then divided them into six groups, each group taking a different paragraph, starting with the second paragraph of the article. In our respective classes we then modeled one process for summarizing, focusing on the first paragraph. Putting the paragraph on an overhead projector, we went through it thinking aloud as we underlined phrases that contained what we thought was the most important information and explaining how we were making our decisions. We then composed a sentence that included the information in the phrases but not copying word for word. This, we explained, was one approach to summarizing a paragraph.

It was then time for the students to tackle their own paragraphs. Working individually, group members first underlined what they considered to be the important phrases in the paragraph assigned to their group. They then shared what they had underlined with the whole group, with members arguing about what to include or exclude until the group agreed on what was essential. Then, working individually once again, each student wrote a sentence that expressed the ideas in these essential phrases without repeating them word for word. After each student had shared his or her sentence with the rest of the group, the group either chose one it felt was the best summary sentence or combined parts from different sentences to come up with a summary sentence acceptable to everyone.

We had already written on the board a summary sentence for the first paragraph, and now each group added its summary sentence, in order, creating a paragraph summarizing the whole article. We explained that the class could test the accuracy of the summary by seeing how well a person who had not read the article could understand its main ideas by reading our newly constructed paragraph. Sometimes we would enlist a passing student or teacher to test the paragraph. Even though these pieced-together summary paragraphs often lacked appropriate transition words and had little elegance or style, the passers-by could usually understand the key ideas of the text the class had read.

In beginning to talk about *how* readers summarize, we generated a list of criteria for "what makes a good summary" with our students. Students commonly said that good summaries were shorter than the original text, contained all the most important information but left out most of the details and examples used in the text to illustrate key points. Once a class had developed a set of criteria for a good summary, we used a variety of other activities to strengthen students' summarizing skills.

Throughout the term we continued to ask students to practice summarizing texts, sometimes on their own and sometimes in class with group support. To ensure that everyone was practicing the strategy, we required each student to underline key chunks of text and write a summary sentence before group sharing.

Working in groups, students heard different perspectives about the information that is and is not considered important. This made them more careful about what they included and what they left out. When they seemed to be having a particularly hard time writing their summaries, we provided scaffolding for them, asking them to think in terms of *signal words* such as *first, then,* and *finally*. Using such words helped students summarize because it gave them a structure into which to fit information. At the end, the group summaries were incorporated into a single summary, and the class tested each section to see if it met the criteria. Summary sections were revised as necessary, and students then copied down the revised version of the whole summary.

Another activity helped students become more conscious of the steps one takes in summarizing and gave them a chance to get feedback from a peer rather than the teacher. We found this lesson design worked well for two reasons: first, struggling students did not feel the teacher was pointing out their faults, and second, students had another chance to feel like experts whose feedback to each other was valuable.

SUMMARY ANALYSIS BY A PEER

Procedure

- Have students read and summarize a text as homework.
- In class, ask each student to draw a line under his or her summary and then trade summaries with a partner.
- Ask students to answer the following questions on their partner's paper, under the line:

  If you hadn't read the text yourself, would you be able to understand what it was about from this summary? Why or why not?

  Is there anything important that should be added to this summary? What is it?

  Is there anything unimportant that could be left out of the summary? What is it?
- Have students return the summaries to their authors and ask them to read the answers to the questions.
- Have students revise their summaries based on the feedback they received.

As always, we asked students to reflect on and share the process they used to summarize a text. This helped them become more metacognitive and evaluate how well their processes were serving them. When we asked students to describe their summarizing processes, we received comments like these: "I read the whole story first. I read parts of the paragraphs second because I wanted to look for more information. I tried to write sentences for each paragraph and I jumped from paragraph to paragraph. I tried to include parts that I thought were important. In my summary I wrote about five sentences." "I read half of the story then I thought it through, then I read the rest. Then I skimmed through it a couple of times to get my memory going. I started putting chunks for every paragraph, from beginning to middle to end. Then I decided to put the important stuff like how he doesn't like reading that I thought were the most important."

Predicting

To introduce the tool of predicting, we once again asked students to focus on something familiar: we asked them about the television news they watched. Most watched some news, often about sports, and they were aware of the different categories of news presented on the typical nightly news show. We asked them to think about all the sections of a news program and identify the one that has a very different function from all the others. After some silliness and wild guessing, one student would identify the weather forecast as being different from news reporting in general. Students saw right away that the weather forecast was a prediction of what might happen whereas other parts of the news reported what had happened. We led a discussion of how meteorologists made predictions using signs and information gathered from weather patterns that had already happened. And although everyone agreed that weather predictions are often incorrect, it turned out that most teachers and students paid attention to them and would take an umbrella or wear an extra sweater—just in case predictions of rain or cold were correct.

We then connected the idea of predicting weather changes based on various signs and prior experiences to the idea of predicting the movements or changes in a text by noting text signals and drawing on prior experiences with reading different types of texts. Like meteorologists' forecasts, predictions made while reading may not always be accurate, but they do prepare readers to encounter ideas or information that may be coming up in the text.

It turned out that most of our students were already familiar with the idea of predicting content from a title or from clues found in narratives. But we wanted them to start using prediction routinely with expository texts, to find clues in the text structure that would help them determine what type of information the author would be presenting next.

To give students practice with anticipating what *moves* an author is about to make—we gave them a list of some of the signal structures, words, and phrases that guide readers as they follow the path of ideas an author has created (Exhibit 5.1).

Using a simple paragraph, we then modeled how a reader might predict what would follow a sentence like this one in a world history book: "There were three main causes of World War I."

Based on their experience of predicting content, some students immediately assumed they should try to guess what the three reasons might be. But once we talked about trying to predict the *type* of information the author would be presenting next, students saw that they needed to prepare themselves to read about these three causes. In this case prediction allowed them to ready a place in their minds for information about "causes of World War I."

We helped students use this prediction technique as they read a range of texts throughout the thematic units. We also had them use the technique on sample reading comprehension sections of SAT exams. As the class went through a close reading of these SAT passages, even we teachers were surprised at the number of signal words found in these often dense excerpts from discipline-based expository texts.

The following activity helped students learn to use clues in the text to prepare themselves for information likely to be coming next. When they

---

EXHIBIT 5.1

Signals for Predicting

Predicting is making guesses based on evidence in the text about what information will be presented next. Predictions help a reader become mentally prepared to understand ideas in a text.

Some Guidelines for Predicting

If the Text Contains These Items	*You Can Probably Expect to Find These Structures*
1. A question	1. An answer
2. A colon (:)	2. A list
3. A headline	3. Information about the headline topic
4. *Therefore*	4. Results or conclusions
5. *That is (i.e.)*	5. A definition
In other words	
Consists of	
Is equal to	
Means	
6. *For example (e.g.)*	6. Example(s)
For instance	
Such as	
Is like	
Including	
To illustrate	
7. *Similarly*	7. A comparison (how things are the same)
In the same way	
Just like	
Just as	
Likewise	
In comparison	
Also	
8. *In contrast*	8. A contrast (how things are different)
On the other hand	
However	
Whereas	
But	
Yet	

---

think of predicting, most students will think of figuring out the culprit in a whodunit movie or noticing the clues that foreshadow how a piece of fiction will turn out. In this activity we made a distinction between predicting the outcome of a text, a *crystal ball* type of prediction, and predicting what the text is preparing the reader for, which we described as *predicting the moves of the text.*

PREDICTING

Materials

A high-interest expository text that has headings, subsections, or other context clues students can use to make predictions (one text we used was an article from *Scope* magazine titled "Going to Extremes," about extreme sports).

Procedure

- Have students fold a piece of paper down the middle lengthwise to make two columns; ask them to write "Information" at the top of the left-hand column and "Prediction" at the top of the right-hand column.
- Tell students you will be giving them pieces of information about an article they will be reading and that they will use this information to predict what the article will address next.
- Ask students to write in the Information column: "Title—'Going to Extremes.'"
- Ask them to write in the Prediction column what prediction about the article's content they would make based on that title.
- Ask some students to volunteer their ideas for the class, and write them on the board, starting a chart. If a student's answer seems odd, ask him or her to explain the thinking behind the prediction.
- In the Information column, have students write "Subtitle—'These Extremely Popular Sports Are Making Some People Extremely Uneasy,'" and then, in the Prediction column, have them make another prediction about the article's content.
- Ask some students to volunteer their answers, and continue to fill in the chart on the board.
- Repeat this process for other subtitles, major headings, pictures, and any other context clues in the article.
- Pass out the article and read it with the class to see how their predictions hold up.

An advantage of this activity is that it gives the teacher a chance to address what happens when a reader makes a incorrect prediction. Oftentimes, students make a connection between something they are learning and something from their schemata. But sometimes the text moves in a different direction than the student expected, and the schema activation turns out not to be advantageous. The danger is that the student will fail to abandon his or her idea of what the text is going to be about and then fail to understand the text, because it does not fit with his or her idea.

In this activity the teacher can refer to the chart on the board and ask students if the early predictions make sense in light of the later information they received. When a prediction no longer makes sense, the teacher crosses it off the chart and tells the students to abandon the idea. For example, students made many different predictions based on the title "Going to Extremes": they thought the article might be about girls who go on crash diets to lose weight and end up becoming anorexic; about extreme sports, like the ones on ESPN;

or about the girl who delivered her baby at the prom and killed it so she could go back to the dance. But when they hear the subtitle "These Extremely Popular Sports Are Making Some People Extremely Uneasy," students see that the second prediction is the only one that remains plausible and that they need to abandon their other ideas and start thinking about the sports theme.

Clarifying

When students come to a part of a text they do not readily understand, they can use various processes for clarifying their understanding. We used the following activity to give students practice in using clarification processes. It also gave us insights into students' thought processes as they read difficult texts. We gave students a definition of *clarifying* and a set of steps to help them build clarifying strategies as follows:

Clarifying: to make the meaning of a text clear or easier to understand by using different comprehension strategies (plans to figure out the meaning).

Steps for clarifying: (1) Ignore and read on if you understand enough to keep going; (2) keep reading to see if the meaning gets clearer; (3) reread what is unclear; (4) reread the section right before what was unclear; (5) connect what you are reading to things you already know or have read before; (6) get outside help.

We helped students develop the habit of clarifying what they do not understand as they read a variety of text through the following activity.

CLARIFYING A TEXT

Procedure

- Have students make the following chart:
  Text   Question or Confusion   Strategy   Clarification
- Assign a text for homework, and have students fill out the chart, noting what they needed to clarify as they read and what strategy they used.
- Go over the charts the next day in class, and discuss the different strategies students used to help themselves out.

Exhibit 5.2 shows how one student worked to clarify passages from *Bless Me, Ultima.*

Not surprisingly, different students will need to clarify different things. For example, some students might have trouble with Spanish words that were not translated into English, and students who understand those words might have trouble understanding relationships between the characters.

EXHIBIT 5.2

Student Work Sample: Clarification Chart

Text	Question or Confusion	Strategy	Clarification
I rushed into the melee	What does he mean?	Ignore	
I heard Ultima's owl sing	I don't understand this	Ignore	
No one knew the Vitamin Kid's name	How come no one knows the Vitamin Kid's name?	Keep reading	He never stopped long enough to talk
La tristesa de la vida	What does this mean?	Re-read right before	Like sorrow or self-pity—lonely
Not even with Horse and Bones	What does he mean by this?	Not outside help	Probably their names like of friends

Source: *Text excerpts from "Seis" in* Bless Me, Ultima *by Rudolfo A. Anaya (New York: Warner Books, 1972), pp. 50–59.*

Discussing students' various difficulties helps the students see that people read and understand things in different ways.

Preparing Students to Lead Their Own Learning

As we moved into our second unit of Academic Literacy, Reading Media, we thought that students might be ready to try out their new skills of questioning, summarizing, predicting, and clarifying on a difficult expository text and that we would use all the steps of the reciprocal teaching process. We chose a challenging article on a topic of interest to students: mass media. The article presented the media as representations of reality that have an audience in mind and an interpretation to communicate. Given the complexity of both its ideas and sentence structures, we knew students would have to work hard to understand it, but we felt they now had the tools to help them do so. Yet when we asked them to read the first paragraph and write five questions that they would likely be able to answer as a result of their reading, they quickly got stuck. Most were unable to come up with even one question. When we tried to locate the root of this comprehension problem, it became clear that the complex sentences and expository style were getting in the way.

Learning to Break It Down: Chunking Difficult Texts

I like chunking because it helps me understand the text little bits at a time, so I can understand the whole thing. Sometimes I'd see a big piece of text

and think, "There's no way I can understand all that!" But if I chunk it,
then it's easy to understand even a big long text.

We had taken for granted that students were breaking complex sentences into shorter phrases as they read as a way to manage their comprehension. Once we raised this possibility, many students realized for the first time that they could pause in a sentence to think, even when no comma or period told them to stop. Much to our surprise, in the end-of-term course evaluation many students cited this practice of reading phrases, or "chunking," as one of the most useful strategies they had learned.

As we always tried to do in talking with students about reading processes and strategies, we used examples close to students' lives. We introduced the concept of chunking and the following activity by talking about pizza. "Even if you're really hungry," we pointed out, "you can't eat a whole pizza at once. You have to eat it a little bit at a time, in slices. Understanding text is similar to eating pizza: though you may want to read a large amount at once, you may not be able to understand it unless you take it in bits and pieces. Depending on the type of text you're reading, you may be able to understand a lot at once or only a little at once."

CHUNKING A TEXT

The purpose of chunking is to give students practice making sense out of a text by breaking it into understandable chunks. Materials needed include a text that explains how to do something (like the explanation of the procedure for doing laundry or how to play a guitar).

Procedure

- Read a text out loud to the class, and then ask students to write down the procedure they think is being described.
- Lead the class in going though the explanation and breaking it down into chunks.
- Help the class piece the components together to figure out what procedure is being described.
- Once they know what is being described, have students do a short description of how they figured it out: when did they understand it, what part of the text was key and why, and so forth.

In class discussions about chunking, we reminded students that the size of each chunk would vary according to the text and the reader: some students might be able to digest large chunks of a particular text, and others might prefer small chunks of the same text. Some texts would not require any chunking. But at the other end of the spectrum, if students found they were breaking text into two- or three-word chunks, that might be a sign that chunking was not going to be an effective strategy for them with that particular text. At that point, we said, they might want to consider the bigger picture: Did they have the necessary background knowledge for understanding the text? Was the vocabulary too difficult? Were they having trouble focusing their attention on the text? We emphasized yet again that they were the experts regarding what was happening in their own minds as they tried to read and that they had to use this expertise to decide which strategy or strategies might help in a given reading situation.

Chunking difficult, complex sentences into smaller, comprehendible phrases was an especially powerful strategy for students who had never been able to "crack the code" of expository language before. One student asked, "Why do they write it this way?" She observed, "It seems like they just want to keep people like us from understanding it—to keep us out." We were able to show her, along with her fellow students, that chunking and analyzing sentences, while effortful, was a way to gain entry into this world.

By late fall we thought that our students had had enough practice with the component parts of reciprocal teaching and were ready to put questioning, summarizing, predicting, and clarifying all together in the full RT process for reading difficult expository texts.

We began the reciprocal teaching activity by explaining the entire RT procedure to students. We also described how RT would take place in a *fishbowl:* a space in the middle of the classroom in which one group of students worked while the rest of the class observed and took notes on what they saw. This would enable all students to observe the RT process in action several times. For those in the fishbowl at the moment, the added pressure of being the focus of attention would result in their taking the procedure seriously.

RECIPROCAL TEACHING IN A FISHBOWL

Procedure

- Make groups for the students that they will work in each time they do RT; put strong readers and struggling readers together in groups.
- Explain the RT procedure to the class. Have students write the procedure down.
  Discussion leader (DL) tells the group which part of the text to read silently.
  DL asks the group two or three questions from the reading.
  DL asks if any group members have questions.
  DL summarizes the text.
  Group members add to the summary.
  DL talks about any part of the text that was confusing and asks the group to help clarify it.
  Group members help each other understand the text.
  Each group member predicts what will come next.

- Make a fishbowl in the middle of the room, and have one group come into it at a time.
- Act as the discussion leader for each group when it first comes into the fishbowl, so that group members see the teacher modeling this role and also experience how the process works; have students outside the circle observe what goes on inside the circle.
- After each group has been in the fishbowl, have each group come in again to work with a different piece of text; this time assign a group member to be the discussion leader.
- After each group has been in the fishbowl twice, address any questions about the procedure, and then let each group work individually with another piece of text, with each person having a chance to be the discussion leader.

Source: A. S. Palinscar and A. L. Brown, "Reciprocal Teaching of Comprehension-Monitoring Activities."

It is also important to understand that the efficacy of an RT group depends on its makeup. Teachers must make the groups as heterogeneous as possible, with stronger and weaker readers in each group. Assign the strongest readers to be the group's first student discussion leaders, so that the struggling readers can see the process working in their group a few times before they have to be the discussion leader. Students can be each other's models for what good readers do; readers of different levels and with different skills learn more from each other in a group than readers with very similar abilities do.

Finally, we reiterate that we used the reciprocal teaching process as a means to an end, not an end in itself. Our goal was not to produce groups of students who could follow the RT procedure perfectly; rather it was to give students opportunities to use their comprehension strategies over and over and so to internalize them.

Moving Toward Independence and Multiple Types of Texts

As students read narratives during Unit One testifying to the power of reading to change lives, expository pieces from *Becoming a Nation of Readers*, and President Clinton's Reading Excellence Act, they continued to question, summarize, predict, and clarify as they worked on their own and in groups to comprehend these texts. These same strategies continued to be an explicit part of the curriculum and of teachers and students' joint inquiry into reading processes, through the Reading Media unit, as students read expository pieces about critical media literacy, watched films about the advertising industry, and analyzed and produced their own advertisements designed to target specific audiences.

In the next chapter we describe the ways students continued to build on the social and personal foundation teachers and students had developed as a community of readers and how they continued to use the strategies in their mental toolbelts and to build specific kinds of text and content knowledge, culminating in reading multiple types of difficult texts in the final unit we taught in the pilot year, Reading History.

Notes

1. This activity is adapted from R. J. Tierney, J. E. Readence, and E. K. Dishner, *Reading Strategies and Practices: A Compendium,* 4th ed. (Needham Heights, Mass.: Allyn & Bacon, 1995), which is adapted from B. Davey, "Think-Aloud: Modeling the Cognitive Processes of Reading Comprehension," *Journal of Reading,* 1983, 27, 184–193.

2. A. S. Palinscar and A. L. Brown, "Reciprocal Teaching of Comprehension-Monitoring Activities." Technical Report No. 269 (Cambridge, Mass.: Bolt, Beranek and Newman, 1983).

3. A. V. Manzo, "Improving Reading Comprehension Through Reciprocal Questioning," unpublished doctoral dissertation, 1968, Syracuse University, cited in Tierney, Readence, and Dishner, *Reading Strategies and Practices.*

4. T. Raphael, "Question-Answering Strategies for Children," *The Reading Teacher,* 1982, 36, 186–190.

5. F. Douglass, *Narrative of the Life of Frederick Douglass, an American Slave* (Boston: Anti-Slavery Office, 1845).

Chapter 6

Building Context, Text, and Disciplinary Knowledge

The doctor specializes in the medical book. He has schema for that kind of text and he might not have schema for law like a lawyer does, but they are both smart; it's just that they don't have the schema for a certain thing.

AS IS TRUE of much about reading, knowledge—whether about the world of ideas in a text or about the ways particular texts work—both supports reading comprehension and develops as a result of reading. In order for students to become proficient at "reading to learn," however, they need to know something about the topics they will encounter in the text to make connections to the ideas and elaborate their prior understandings. And in order for students to access different types of texts, they need to know how to read the conventions (the signposts authors leave) that direct the reader through the author's ideas. To make sense of disciplinary texts in subject area classes, students also need to know about the customary ways of thinking, and therefore reading, that constitute the practice of science, history, math, and literature.

In the sections that follow, we describe activities we used in Academic Literacy to develop students' knowledge of content and of texts. The last section of this chapter describes a thematic unit in which students made use of content and text knowledge in the context of exploring the particular discourse of the discipline of history.

Thinking Metacognitively About Prior Knowledge

Many teachers have long recognized the importance of background knowledge to students' understanding of new information and ideas, including those introduced in texts. When giving reading assignments, most teachers take it upon themselves to provide students with background knowledge about the topic or text type or to somehow evoke students' own prior knowledge. What teachers do less often is help students think metacognitively about prior knowledge, showing them how they can activate relevant knowledge they have already developed from other reading, from past discussions, and from experience and demonstrating how they can further develop this existing knowledge in preparation for reading a new text.

In the Academic Literacy course, we made the role of background knowledge an integral topic in our collaborative inquiry with students into reading. Early in the school year we began exploring why prior knowledge is important when a reader is trying to make sense of text. We introduced the word *schema* to describe a network of associated knowledge that an individual has gathered and organized in his or her head.

As early as the first day of the class, while reading Abbott and Costello's famous routine "Who's on First," students had encountered the concept of a schema and the role of prior knowledge in understanding. After discussing the joke in "Who's on First," we asked students to identify what prior knowledge about the world and about language a listener would need in order to understand the routine. They decided a listener would need to know the basic rules of baseball and also something about naming practices in the English language. The listener would need to recognize that "Who," "What," and "I Don't Know" (names of baseball players in the routine) are not common names for people and that is why Costello can't understand what Abbott is saying when he insists that Who's on first base, What's on second, and I Don't Know is on third.

We tried to further clarify the concept that individuals routinely rely on schemata by using the analogy of a large discount warehouse chain. Because almost all the students had been to at least one discount warehouse, we were able to talk with them about how you can usually find your way around these cavernous stores quite easily because, even though they stock thousands of disparate items, these items are organized into sections according to some basic categories and subcategories. You can always count on a food section; a book, music, and video section; a computer section; an appliance section; and so forth. This organization makes it considerably easier to find what you are looking for. Instead of wandering the aisles hoping to find frozen ravioli, for instance, you can go directly to the grocery section and within that to the frozen food section and within that to the frozen dinners section and grab it.

We then explained that even though people's brains can store more information than there are products in a warehouse store, individuals do not always store their information in a way that allows them to easily retrieve it. Students came to see that building and activating a schema was a way to organize information in their brains, a way to connect pieces of related knowledge in their heads.

Another activity we used to further explore the role of prior knowledge in making sense of text was to read and discuss humorous, ambiguous headlines, for example, "Red Tape Holds Up Bridge." Students observed that without an appropriate schema, someone might think this headline was about a bridge held together with lots of brightly colored tape. What is needed to understand this headline, of course, is the knowledge that *red tape* is a euphemism for bureaucracy. Jointly considering a variety of similarly ambiguous headlines helped students see for themselves that prior knowledge played a significant role in how easily or accurately they interpreted text.

AMBIGUOUS HEADLINES

Materials

Newspaper headlines that can be interpreted in more than one way (for example: "Police Begin Campaign to Run Down Jaywalkers," "Safety Experts Say School Bus Passengers Should be Belted," "Two Sisters Reunited After 18 Years in Checkout Counter," "Kids Make Nutritious Snacks," "New Vaccine May Contain Rabies," "Killer Sentenced to Die for Second Time in 10 Years," and "Miners Refuse to Work After Death").

Procedure

- Have students copy down an ambiguous headline.
- Ask them to write what they believe to be an improbable but plausible explanation based on a literal reading of the words.
- Ask them to write what they believe to be the correct explanation of what it means.
- Ask them to write an explanation of the schema necessary to understand the correct meaning.

Here is part of one student's list of definitions.

Headline Hunt

1. *Iraqi Head Seeks Arms.*

   Wrong meaning: A person who only has a head is looking for some arms.

   Correct meaning: The leader of Iraq wants weapons.

   Schema: You have to know that head can mean leader and arms can mean weapons.

2. *Squad Helps Dog Bite Victim*

   Wrong meaning: Bad people help a dog bite people.

   Correct meaning: A group of people rescue the people who got bitten by dogs.

   Schema: You have to know that groups of rescuers are sometimes called squads.

3. *Eye Drops Off Shelf*

   Wrong meaning: The eye falls down off the shelf.

   Correct meaning: Eyedrop medicine gets removed from the store.

   Schema: You have to know that headlines sometimes leave out words to save space—"Eye Drops Taken Off Shelves" would have made more sense—and that when something is wrong, stuff gets taken out of the store so it doesn't hurt someone.

We routinely started class with an ambiguous headline or two. We found this a lively way to engage students in exploring background knowledge and its influences on comprehension. We also enlisted students in the hunt for headlines or other text examples demonstrating this concept.

Different Kinds of Knowledge

One activity we used frequently to build or activate students' relevant schemata before starting a text or a unit was Give One, Get One, developed by Kate Kinsella.[1] This collaborative activity served two purposes: it raised students' awareness about the relevant content knowledge they already had and it increased that knowledge. The process generated a web of interconnected ideas, knowledge, and experience to help students consider what they would subsequently learn from the text.

▌	**GIVE ONE, GET ONE**

Procedure

- Have students fold a piece of paper lengthwise to form two columns and write "Give One" at the top of the left-hand column and "Get One" at the top of the right-hand column.
- Have students brainstorm a list of all the things they already know about the topic they will be studying, writing the items down in the left column.
- After they make the list, have them talk to other students about what is on their lists.
- Have students write any new information they get from these discussions in the right column of their lists, along with the name of the person who gave them the information
- Once everyone has given and gotten information, have the whole class discuss the information students have listed.
- Again, have students write any new information they get from this discussion in the right column of their lists.

We did this activity periodically before starting to study a subject that students were likely to have some knowledge about already. Whether they realize it or not, students appreciate being able to show what they already know about something. As students brainstormed their individual lists, we circulated around the room and provided some information or ideas for students who were struggling to come up with any on their own. That way, when it was time for students to circulate and share information, no one had an empty list.

We also discussed students' final lists of information with the aim of making sure they were accurate. Sometimes, as in the following example of one student's list, students may have factually faulty content knowledge; it was important that they discard any incorrect information before we started the unit.

Give One, Get One

Ten Things I Know About Malcolm X

1. *He was shot during a speech.*

2. *Born in 1925.*

3. *He had a wife and child.*

4. *Black father, white mother.*

5. ~~*Wrote an autobiography.*~~

6. *He's a famous African American.*

7. *He was a Muslim.*

   8. *He was a good student.*

   9. *He's smart.*

   10. ~~*He freed slaves.*~~

Text Knowledge

Clearly, when making sense of text readers draw not just on their knowledge about the world as it relates to the text—content knowledge—but on their knowledge about typical text structures and vocabulary as well. We helped students learn to pay attention to *text schemata*—the kinds of text structures and language cues that give readers information about text meaning. For example, as described in the previous chapter, we developed lessons to help students become more aware of the kinds of signal words, such as *furthermore* or *however,* that enable readers to make informed predictions about where a text is going.

   We also explored some larger text elements and structures readers can identify and use to comprehend the different texts they encounter. For example, in the Reading Self and Society unit, students read an excerpt from Claude Brown's autobiography. We asked them to consider both the title of the excerpt, "I Heard a Knock at the Door," and the illustration in the text, which showed a policeman approaching the door of an apartment, and to make some assumptions about what they would be reading. Previewing the title and illustrations helped students not only to predict what the story might be about but to build a web of their own related ideas, knowledge, and experience that they could later connect to ideas presented in the text.

   As implied in the name Academic Literacy, one of our major course goals was for students to become comfortable and competent readers of nonfiction, informational texts. In the Reading Self and Society unit, students had struggled to varying degrees with the narrative texts—both fiction and nonfiction—that made up the bulk of our reading. But as a group, they had the most trouble with one of the few expository texts we used during that unit, an essay from *Becoming a Nation of Readers.* In the subsequent Reading Media unit, they had similar troubles with another expository essay, "Critical Media Literacy."

   We decided to capitalize on the ways *cloze passages* could build student familiarity with text structures and vocabulary as well as increase their comprehension skills. In these passages, some words have been omitted, and students are asked to supply words that would make sense in these spaces. Cloze passages are sometimes used to assess students' reading levels in particular kinds of texts. Cloze activities have been shown to improve student reading comprehension as well.

We wanted to use them to help students become more familiar and comfortable with the various language structures of exposition. We found a series of high-interest biographical articles about popular media and sports figures that were written in expository style for *Scope,* published by *Scholastic,* a teen-oriented national magazine. The magazine editors had turned these articles into cloze passages by strategically omitting key words. Readers were to choose appropriate words to fill the blanks from words in a box at the end of the passage. As described in the following activity, we turned these magazine articles into a competitive game, blanking out the boxed word choices, and asking students to come up with words on their own.

CLOZE PASSAGES

Materials

High-interest cloze passages, either a ready-made cloze text or an article of interest to students that you have retyped, omitting every fifth word.

Procedure:

- Have students read the passage and try to determine from context the words that might fit in the blanks.
- Explain to students that they will receive five points for getting a word the author used and three points for coming up with another word that makes sense in the context.
- Once everyone has made some choices, read through the passage as a class, go over the right answers, and award points as earned. Have students ask if other words they chose will fit, and tell them whether those words get points or not.
- Have students total up their points, and declare one or more winners.
- Discuss why some words don't fit in certain blanks, letting students explain the reasons to each other whenever possible.

We did this activity periodically to give students some practice in understanding new vocabulary words from clues in a sentence and to help them become more aware of how words fit together; oftentimes students come up with the right word in the wrong form. Through repeated opportunities like these, students could improve their understanding of some of the differences between parts of speech, verb tenses, and so forth when they heard why their words did not fit.

In addition, this activity helps prepare students for the Degrees of Reading Power test (see Appendix B) that we give them at the beginning and the end of the year and that contains cloze passages. Doing this activity in class helps them become familiar with the kinds of questions they will see on the test.

These activities with vocabulary and cloze passages reinforced students' understanding of the different types of language proficient readers must be familiar with. In addition to enjoying the competition of the game and the content of the articles, students began to understand that certain types of words and sentence structures were characteristic of particular kinds of texts.

Word Knowledge

We often found students struggling with unfamiliar vocabulary. We could simply have determined what words we thought students needed to know if they were to understand a particular text, but we wanted not only to support their vocabulary building but also to maintain the spirit of inquiry and collaboration characterizing a reading apprenticeship classroom. So we asked students to work in groups to identify what we called *survival words*—those words a reader would have to know in order to have his or her comprehension survive while reading a particular text. By identifying only survival words, students came to understand that they could often comprehend a passage without knowing every word. They also learned to identify words key to understanding a text, becoming more aware of when they should turn to resources such as other readers or dictionaries to clarify understanding. Students did not have to know the meaning of a word in order to identify it as a survival word.

We used the following activity to prepare students for possibly difficult vocabulary. It worked well because among themselves the students in a class usually know at least the approximate meaning of many words, so they can help each other out with definitions. Once again, this gave students a chance to feel like experts, and it reinforced the feeling of community in the classroom.

Like comprehension itself, word knowledge is not an all-or-nothing proposition. As all readers know from their own experience, readers are often somewhat familiar with a word, even if they cannot define it specifically. Similarly, even when they do not have prior knowledge of a word, they may be able to derive its meaning from context. This activity gets this idea across to students and helps them explore and expand their vocabularies.

SURVIVAL WORDS

Procedure

- From a text you will be teaching, choose several words that may trip students up and that students are likely to see again or use a list of survival words that students have generated.
- Have students make a chart that has the following column headings:
  Word   A   B   C   D   Meaning
- Have students copy each word down in the first column of the chart and check the appropriate A, B, C, or D category for each word:
  A. I know the meaning, and I use the word.
  B. I know the meaning, but I don't use the word
  C. I've seen the word before, but I don't really know it.
  D. I've never seen the word before.
- Ask students to write the meanings of as many of the words as they know in the Meaning column.
- After students have rated their word knowledge and written their meanings, break them into groups and ask them to share with each other the meanings they are most confident about.
- Then go over their charts with them, answer any questions, and give them additional information about or help them clarify words with which they still have difficulty.

It is important not to use too many words in any one session of this activity. The goal is for students to learn and retain the words that will be key to making sense of a class text rather than memorize lists of words. Six to ten key words is ample. We took this collaborative approach to building word knowledge as our classrooms read different texts throughout the year.

Disciplinary Knowledge: The Reading History Unit

Throughout Academic Literacy, we circled back to the idea that readers draw on prior knowledge when trying to understand new knowledge in academic texts. But it was in the Reading History unit that students had the greatest opportunities to experience the true power of prior knowledge in helping a reader master new ideas and information. We conceived the Reading History unit because we felt the need to familiarize our freshmen students with some of the different types of history texts they would be expected to read throughout high school. In designing the unit, we hoped students' high hopes for a peaceful and just society in the twenty-first century would be a motivation for them to read history, with its lessons from the past. Students would be asked to address the complex questions of what forces drive acts of injustice and how individuals and societies might prevent future injustices. In taking on this challenging task they would be expected to draw on their growing understanding of themselves as readers, to use the cognitive strategies they had learned, and to participate in a collaborative inquiry process. We discuss the Reading History unit here to show the many ways important aspects of reading instruction can be embedded in subject area instruction without losing the primary focus on teaching students discipline-specific ways of thinking and on building students' subject area knowledge.

"Reading to Learn" in the Reading History Unit
Building Motivation and New Conceptions of History

We began by asking students to write their answer to this question: "What comes to mind when you think of reading history?" Many students chronicled an experience marked by carrying and studying large, heavy textbooks; memorization of facts and dates; and most of all, boredom. As one young woman wrote, "When I think about studying history, the things that come to mind are boring facts and memorizing dates. I think of a boring teacher and big (huge) textbooks and endless nights of studying, outlining, cramming, etc."

Getting students' general disinterest in history and their boredom with its texts out on the table allowed us to acknowledge and address that prior experience. Hearing their views about history gave us an important starting place for building a more elaborate concept of the discipline. Students thought history was dates and events and famous people; we needed to help them see it instead as a discipline of study to explain and interpret the past.

We invited students to reconsider their notions of history. As a prompt we gave them Santayana's famous dictum: "Those who cannot remember the past are condemned to repeat it." We asked them, first, to paraphrase what they thought Santayana was saying and, then, to respond with their own opinion. As an entry point to a unit about injustice, intolerance, and intergroup hatred, Santayana's view confronted our diverse ninth graders with a new concept and rationale for the academic discipline of history.

To help students begin making connections between the past, which they would read about in the various texts of the unit, and the present, which they knew from personal experience, we had them work in groups to brainstorm associations with some key conceptual vocabulary, including *persecution, racism, prejudice, stereotype, victim,* and *tolerance.* Each group was given its own key word and asked to make a list, or map, of other words and ideas this key word brought to mind. Each student wrote his or her own associations independently, then shared them within the group. By comparing the different lists its members had made, the group then worked toward an agreed-upon definition.

For our particular urban students, these key words triggered a wealth of personal and familial experiences. This activity helped them make personal connections to the topic of study, bring to the surface their prior knowledge about related ideas and experiences, explore conceptual vocabulary, and see that history itself might be about much more than facts and figures.

Throughout the Reading History unit, students were engaged in a variety of activities that built their history-related content knowledge and text schemata. Course texts thus served multiple purposes. They tapped students' prior knowledge and interest in the topic of study, they offered opportunities to build student awareness of text and language structures in expository texts, and they provided opportunities for students to come to understand history as interpretation of historical events rather than a collection of facts.

Building Expository Text Schema Through Previewing and Graphic Organizers

To help students understand their history texts, we provided some specific tools for organizing their thinking about texts and also introduced them to the concept of *previewing.* After we had generated some discussion about the key concepts of the unit, we gave students an article about current hate crimes in America. Our goal was twofold: to continue to connect the present with the past, thereby motivating students' interest in history, and to further build students' knowledge of and ability to work with expository text structures.

We teachers had already read the hate crimes article and determined that it was structured around five topics: examples of hate crimes, a definition of a hate crime, characteristics of hate crimes, causes of hate crimes, and conclusions. To help students understand how the text was organized, we introduced a graphic organizer in the form of a tree, with prior knowledge as roots, the main topic as the trunk, and these five topics as the branches (Figure 6.1).

FIGURE 6.1

Student Work Sample: Tree Organizer for Hate Crimes Article

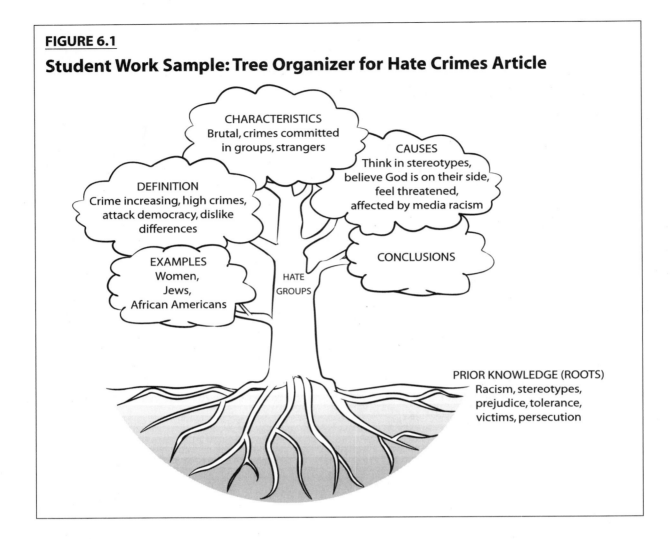

TREES (GRAPHIC ORGANIZERS)

Materials

A nonfiction text that has a lot of information about a single subject.

Procedure

- Explain to students that a graphic organizer is a way to organize notes into some kind of chart or picture.
- Tell them that one form of graphic organizer is the tree, and that they will be using a tree to organize notes about this text.
- Explain to them that certain kinds of information go in certain places on the tree:

  On the trunk: name of the text upon which the notes are based

  On the roots: any schemata you have about the subject you are reading about

  On the branches: the main categories of information in the text

  On the leaves: individual facts about a given section of the text

- Create a tree on the board and have students supply the information to be filled in on the trunk; have students copy this tree down.
- Ask students to volunteer any information they have about the topic, and put that information on the roots of the tree.
- Have students read the first part of the text as a class, and help students figure out what each branch of the tree should be; then fill in each branch on the tree.
- Put students in groups, and assign each group one branch of the tree. Each groups reads its section of the text and chooses three to five pieces of information that should be leaves on the tree.
- Have the members of each group present their information to the class and add their leaves to the tree on the board, and have the class copy all the leaves.
- Discuss the text based on the notes on the tree.

As our students read their article, they added detail to the tree with both smaller branches and leaves. This way of organizing the text information graphically gave students a way to sort out and depict main ideas and supporting details. They continued to use this form of graphic organizer as they read other texts throughout the unit.

The central text for the unit was "Totalitarianism in the Modern World," a chapter from a thematically organized ancillary text for the tenth-grade world history curriculum.[2] This chapter began with theories from psychologists, sociologists, and political scientists about the roots of human aggression and intolerance. We showed students how to *preview* the chapter by reading not only the chapter title, headings, and illustrations, but also the guiding questions and glossary presented at the end of the chapter. From this preview, students drew a tree of the main ideas, as they had done for the hate crimes article. Teacher and students then read some of the chapter together and added details to the tree. Here, too, the use of a graphic organizer helped students see how information was structured in the text and also how they might organize and keep track of their own thoughts as they read.

The next section of the chapter discussed the relationship among individual aggression, group aggression, and government power and politics. At this point we introduced another graphic organizer, a Venn diagram to help students see how these interacting forces could result in genocide.

As we worked through the first few sections of the chapter, we noticed that students easily bogged down in the dense amount of detail offered about every historical event mentioned. We wanted students to understand historical writing as an interpretation of historical events, not as a collection of facts, and to see the line of exposition as an author's construction. To highlight this idea, we asked students, working in groups, to take one paragraph from a section of the text and either find or write the one sentence that best captured the most important thing in the paragraph.

When these sentences were put on the board, they helped students see the author's line of reasoning and overall presentation of ideas. We told students it is often difficult to "see the forest for the trees" when reading and had them explain how that particular idiomatic expression was connected to their experience of reading the history textbook.

We also showed students a variety of ways to manage density of information in this type of text. They kept a timeline showing when different events occurred, located countries and events on maps, and filled out charts with important information about the different times in recent history when government-sanctioned group aggression had occurred.

Building Content Knowledge Through Extensive Reading of Multiple Texts

As noted earlier, identifying the topic of a text before reading that text allows the reader to call up appropriate prior knowledge to connect to the ideas in the text. Connecting the *known* to the *new* in this way helps a reader build new knowledge. Reading multiple texts about the same topic is another important way to enrich and build knowledge. In these multiple texts, a reader repeatedly encounters similar ideas and vocabulary, which plant these concepts and words more firmly in his or her mind, but they are presented differently, through different examples and with different connections made for the reader.

With this in mind, we began the history unit with what we thought of as *foundation texts,* specifically, the article on hate crimes and the textbook chapter on totalitarianism. Our intention was to introduce additional texts as students moved toward a culminating project on the Holocaust. We soon discovered, however, that despite the detailed preparation we had given them about how these kinds of texts work, students clearly were not well enough prepared to read and comprehend the history textbook chapter. The amount of background information necessary to make sense of the chapter proved overwhelming to our students. We needed to do more. We began a search for additional print texts and also visual "texts" that could help students make stronger personal connections to the importance and relevance of the issues we wanted them to study. We also wanted ways to provide more of the conceptual and factual knowledge necessary to sustain readers through the hard work of reading a challenging text.

One activity we did to build students' knowledge through multiple texts was the News Portfolio Project. This activity gave students new kinds of texts to read and also a means of making ongoing and explicit connections of the past to the present. Here is how we presented this activity to our students.

NEWS PORTFOLIO PROJECT

Instructions

As part of our unit on history and current events, we will be looking at several newspaper and magazine articles over the next few weeks. For this project you will be reading the newspaper or a news-oriented magazine and collecting articles that relate to the themes we will be investigating. Though we will most likely have a few copies of the paper in class each day, we won't have enough for everyone, so you'll need to find newspapers on your own. You will also need to collect articles over spring break.

Over the next few weeks, you will need to read a newspaper or news magazine several times a week and look for articles that somehow relate to the history unit we are working on. The articles can be about anything from stereotypes to hate crimes to scapegoating to prejudice. If you have a question about whether an article fits this unit, show it to me, and I'll help you figure it out. The idea is to start keeping track of what's happening in the world around you and to start making connections between things that happened in the past and what is going on currently.

Procedure

- Find a relevant article from a newspaper or magazine.
- Cut it out.
- Glue or tape it to a piece of notebook paper.
- Cite the source (that means write down the name of the newspaper or magazine and the date the article appeared).
- Write a one- to two-paragraph summary of the article (this can be done on the back of the notebook paper if the article takes up the whole page).
- Write one to two paragraphs about how the article relates to what we are studying (this can also be done on the back).
- Continue collecting articles until you have met the requirements for the portfolio.
- Just before you turn in the portfolio, you will need to write a one- to two-page paper about how the articles you have collected fit together and about what you have learned in the process of collecting them. I will give you more details about this when we get closer to the due date.

Project Specifics

- Collect a total of five (5) articles for the portfolio.
- All five articles and your introductory paper will be due on Monday, April 12. You have about three and a half weeks to complete the portfolio, so if you read the paper every day, you will definitely be able to find plenty of articles for the project. But if you leave the project until the last minute, you may have a very difficult time finishing on time. *Be advised that you will need to work on this over spring break; if you are going on vacation to another city, read the local paper there, and clip articles to bring home.*
- Newspapers you might look through: *The San Francisco Chronicle, The San Francisco Examiner, The Bay Guardian, SF Weekly, The Oakland Tribune, The San Jose Mercury News, The Independent.*
- Magazines you might look through: *Time, Newsweek, US News and World Report, The New Yorker, Vanity Fair, Harper's, Rolling Stone, Vibe.*

In addition to doing this project, the Academic Literacy classes read the screenplay for Arthur Miller's *The Crucible*. Once again we asked students to look at the ways in which members of a group can become targeted as scapegoats. We discussed the historical context of the play and its connection to McCarthyism. Finally, we showed students a documentary about the genocide of the Armenians by their Turkish rulers in the early 1920s, bringing us back to the chapter on totalitarianism that they had resisted reading. Students were now more knowledgeable about and aware of the terrible consequences of allowing extreme antidemocratic movements to grow. We read with them through the chapter, helping them use text structures as clues and graphic organizers as means of tracking and understanding the causes, examples, and consequences of totalitarianism in the twentieth century.

Thinking and Acting Like Historians: The Holocaust Detective Project

We now felt students were ready to bring together all the knowledge they had built throughout the course—knowledge about content and text structure, cognitive strategies, the value of collaboration, and the relevance of mastering texts to meet their goals for society and for themselves. With their growing confidence as readers, they were ready to embark on a six-week project that would explore the Holocaust. Our goal with what we called the Holocaust History Detective Project was to help students try on disciplinary ways of thinking in order to interpret and explain the historical events of the Holocaust, given what they had learned throughout the Reading History unit.

We began, as we always did, with the assumption that students already knew a lot about what they were going to study. To make that knowledge visible and have students share it, we did the Give One, Get One activity with them with the Holocaust as the topic. Many students had some knowledge about the Holocaust, developed from a variety of sources. They might have read *The Diary of Anne Frank*, seen *Schindler's List*, or heard stories from a family member who survived it.

After students shared what they already knew, we created a list of questions that addressed contradictory pieces of information that students were bringing to the study. Were the Jews the only people to be put into concentration camps? Did Hitler escape from Germany? Did the German people know what was going on in the concentration camps? Were the Nazis a socialist party? How could people tell who was Jewish and who wasn't? Did any Germans try to stop Hitler?

We asked students to hold on to these questions, explaining that we didn't know the answers to some of them and that others were still the subject of ongoing debate among historians. We talked about history as an inquiry into the past in which events had to be reconstructed and interpreted based on various texts and artifacts. We told students that they would work in groups to investigate one aspect of the Holocaust, using a variety of sources as evidence for any conclusions they drew.

When expecting students to read difficult academic texts, we had learned to pay constant attention to their interests and motivation. So before beginning the Historical Investigation Project, we showed students the film *Swing Kids.* This film is based on the true story of resistance to the Hitler youth movement by a group of teenagers who admired the individuality of American culture as they experienced it through the American swing music they loved. Our students were totally engaged, and they identified with the conflict the main character faced between his individual integrity and the pressures a totalitarian system placed on him, his friends, and his family. This film led to discussions of loyalty, courage, rebellion, and idealism—all of which helped students better identify with the time, place, and people they would be studying in their historical investigation.

Interpreting Historical Documents

Our students were now ready to begin their shared inquiry into an aspect of the Holocaust. We divided them into groups of four or five, and each group was assigned one of seven topics: Germany and anti-Semitic laws; concentration camps; non-Jews in concentration camps; Warsaw Ghetto uprising; resistance and escape; protests; and rescues. For each topic, we had prepared a folder containing six to ten relevant historical documents. They were both primary and secondary source materials, including newspaper clippings from the period, translations of official German documents, interviews, excerpts from texts at varying reading levels, photographs, maps, diaries, flow charts, and medical reports on death rates and causes of death, among others. Students were to work with the materials, both individually and with their groups, in order to become experts on their topic.

This historical investigation called on students to read and take notes on a variety of texts and summarize documents and then to create visual representations of important ideas, organize oral presentations of material, and write from different points of view based on the information they had learned. With our support and guidance, students were in fact thinking and acting like apprentice historians, both explaining and interpreting historical events. The knowledge they presented was the result of a collaborative inquiry through which they became the experts on their topic.

Because one of our goals with the Reading History unit was to assist students in learning to *read to learn,* we assessed both their knowledge about the unit and their strategies for accessing this knowledge. In this culminating unit we were pleased to see a good number of our students making use of strategies they had been learning and using throughout the year, as this student comment demonstrates: "When our teacher was helping us pick out main points she used a series on the Holocaust. It just so happens that now I am a lawyer for my final project for the Holocaust. I am defending myself. Another member of the group is supposed to be Henry Himmler. I am going to have my other attorney cross examine me. Now, I just pick out main points. I have this thick book and I found about three paragraphs I could use. I didn't want to read the whole book. But I knew what I wanted to find. When they say Himmler gave the order to kill so many Jews . . . I don't want that for my side because I am trying to get him off. So I knew what I wanted so when I read it, I highlighted it more in my head."

Their grades were based on project presentations and on a learning log of activities they kept throughout the unit. In addition, in a final exam students were asked to demonstrate mastery of content and strategies for accessing this content by interpreting a passage from the textbook that they had not previously read. Finally, they were given a cloze test on the key conceptual vocabulary of the unit. At the end of the year many students told us in their course evaluations that they had learned not only how to read and understand texts better but also about important topics of history. In the spring of the following year, students now in the tenth grade told us how important the history unit had been and how much they still valued from their experience of reading—and interpreting—history.

Notes

1. K. Kinsella, "Initiating ESL Students to the Cooperative College Classroom," *Cooperative Learning and College Teaching,* 5(3), 6–10.

2. L. S. Krieger and K. Neill (eds.), "Totalitarianism in the Modern World," in *Issues of the Modern Age* (D.C. Heath, 1994).

Chapter 7

Embedding Apprenticeship Strategies in Subject Area Classrooms

> My greatest success this year? I'd say it was bringing texts back into the course, rather than just letting them sit on the shelf. It was teaching them the skills to understand it rather than just ignoring it and spoon-feeding the content to them.
>
> Middle school history teacher

THE READING APPRENTICESHIP approach has been successful in developing student reading not only in the stand-alone Academic Literacy course but also in the middle and high school subject area courses taught by teachers in the Strategic Literacy Network. Originally a network of teachers of English, social studies, and English as a second language (ESL), the network has expanded to include teachers of math and science. Students in network classes in these various disciplinary areas are becoming more strategic and confident readers of the texts they encounter.

Network teachers laid the ground for this success in a number of ways: the most important was by conducting inquiries into their own reading processes and sharing their work with one another through interactive workshops and informal, collegial discussions. In the process of integrating new approaches to teaching reading, these teachers came to understand that helping students become independent, critical readers of subject area texts is not a *diversion* from real teaching. Rather it is essential to students' understanding of curriculum content.

A network middle school history, science, and English/language arts teacher put it this way: "Explicit reading instruction early in the year leads to greater student competence. The increase in competence supports subject area work later. The payoff is greater than the initial investment."

This chapter describes the various ways Strategic Literacy Network subject area teachers found to incorporate into their discipline-specific courses the attitudes and activities that are essential to the success of reading apprenticeships—and in the process, to bring reading back into the classroom.

Starting the Metacognitive Conversation

Like Academic Literacy teachers, network subject area teachers invite their students to join them in a collaborative inquiry into the reading process. In disciplinary classes, however, that inquiry delves into reading as it relates to the particular discipline at hand, whether history, science, math, or English. The vehicle for inquiry is an ongoing metacognitive conversation, in which both the teacher as master reader and students as reading apprentices attempt to make visible their processes of puzzling through texts.

For example, one middle school history teacher begins the metacognitive conversation in her classroom by asking students not only "*What* did you find out in your reading?" but also "*How* did you figure that out?" "*How* did you get that idea?" and "*How* did you reach that conclusion?" She teaches her students what the word *metacognition* means and how being metacognitive can help them with problem-solving tasks; she encourages her students to "show off" to older siblings by asking them about their metacognitive processes.

This history teacher found that in the interactive history curriculum her district has adopted, there were few opportunities for students to read extended texts. To help students develop their reading of history texts she began copying and passing out excerpts of the teacher's guide—background information written about each unit of study. She introduced the process of being metacognitive about reading by putting a text up on an overhead projector and then "thinking on paper" as she read, making her own reading process visible to her students.

Thereafter, she had students think on paper as they read these background materials—writing notes in the margins about what they were thinking, questioning, or not understanding. Afterward, students usually met in groups of four to share their reading processes and to clarify vocabulary, ideas, and responses to the text. In full-class discussion the teacher then continued the think-aloud by having students question her about the reading. Often she shared her own thinking on paper, again by writing on an overhead transparency while students read their copies.

Throughout the course, these class discussions focused both on *what* information, conclusions, or questions students drew from their reading and on *how* they went about their reading to make sense of the texts. Other network teachers have developed various approaches to thinking on paper as a way to engage students in metacognitive conversation, first with themselves as they work to understand the text and then with the class. ESL teachers found this approach particularly helpful for their English language learners because it gave these students time to reflect and articulate their reading processes and comprehension problems before taking part in small-group or class discussions.

For students to willingly engage in such revealing public conversation and to do the other hard work that goes along with improving their reading, they must be motivated and they must feel safe. Network teachers have developed a number of ways to support the personal and social dimensions of a reading apprenticeship approach to learning.

The Personal Dimension: Helping Students Find Reasons to Read

Students rarely have any choice over what they are expected to learn in content area classes and therefore few opportunities and little reason to consider what aspects of science, history, or literature might interest them more than others. Hoping to spark students' interest in their own reading processes and, in time, to engender greater student engagement when reading, network teachers have found ways to give students as much choice as possible in their content-related reading. Some network teachers have made opportunities not just to give students more choice but to assist students in developing and expanding their taste in text genres and topics.

In literature classes, for example, several network teachers have developed *literature circles*[1] to allow groups of students to choose a novel they will read, set the schedule and group expectations for completing the novel, and still meet the teacher's goals for student learning (Exhibit 7.1 describes the tools one teacher is developing to manage literature circles). This teacher holds her literature circles accountable for reading by having one group at a time, in a fishbowl (as described in Chapter Five), discuss the book they are reading as the rest of the class observes. The observing students rate the discussion according to criteria the teacher and class have developed. This teacher has found that students in a literature circle often hold one another accountable for completing the reading so that the fishbowl discussions will go well.

<u>**EXHIBIT 7.1**</u>

Circular Logic: Why Literature Circles Don't Have To Drive Teachers Crazy

For the past two years at my high school, I have dedicated much of the last nine-week term of the course Ethnic Literature to literature circles. The idea of four or five novels being read simultaneously by different groups in one class terrified me, but I chose to face my fear, for these reasons:

- My students' reading levels differed widely (CTBS [Comprehensive Tests of Basic Skills] scores indicated a third- to eleventh-grade range).
- My school lacked class sets of novels for my course.
- I wanted my ninth graders to take more responsibility for their own education.
- I was given a free box of books for literature circles.
- People in the Strategic Literacy Initiative talked about literature circles working.

The following materials might be considered a starter kit for literature circles.

TIME MANAGEMENT TOOLS

Student Tools

I gave each group, or circle, a calendar and a due date for finishing the novel. On the calendar, I crossed out any days on which students would not be able to read the novel in class. I then asked them to assign and write on the calendar weekly, or even daily, benchmarks for their reading. All circle members signed the calendar, as if it were a contract.

I created a big calendar for the whole class that showed these student-generated benchmarks. Once a week each group reassessed its progress and changed benchmark dates as needed.

Teacher Tool

I created a weekly schedule of activities for the ninety-minute class periods. For example:

- Monday
  Read in groups
  Triple-entry journal
- Tuesday
  Read in groups
  Triple-entry journal
  Big-group project; group comprehension activity
- Wednesday
  Read in groups
  Triple-entry journal
- Thursday
  Discussions
- Friday
  Read in groups
  Triple-entry journal
  Presentations

SURVEYS

I asked students to fill out a survey before they began literature circles, to help them start to think about their reading behavior. They completed another survey after they had finished a book.

Prereading Survey

Respond to the following questions by circling all the answers that apply.

1. Which of the following do you read on your own?

Book	Magazine	Newspaper
Comic	Manual or liner notes	Other (please explain)

2. How do you decide what you read?

Friend recommends	Family member recommends	Author's name
Topic or type	Review in media	Cover or photos
Other (please explain)		

3. What type of book are you most likely to choose to read?

Romance	Mystery	Action
Horror	Biography or autobiography	Drama
Other (please explain)		

4. How do you usually read?

Silently	Out loud	Someone else reads to me

5. Which way of reading helps you understand the best?

Silently	Out loud	Someone else reads to me

6. What was the last book you read?

   Title:

   Author:

7. Do you have a favorite book? A favorite author?

Postreading Survey

1. Would you recommend this book to a friend?

Yes	No	Depends (please explain)

2. How much of this book did you read (be honest)?

All of it	Most of it	Half of it
Some of it	None of it	

3. When you're assigned a book that the whole class reads, how much do you usually read?

All of it	Most of it	Half of it
Some of it	None of it	

4. When you choose a book to read on your own, how much do you usually read?

All of it	Most of it	Half of it
Some of it	I don't read on my own	

5. What did you think about choosing your own book?

Liked choosing	Didn't like choosing (please explain)

6. What were your favorite parts of literature circles (circle no more than three)?

Choosing the book	Making the calendar	Reading in class
Keeping a journal	Fishbowl discussions	Movie poster
Talk show	Vocabulary in context	

7. What were your least favorite parts of literature circles (circle no more than three)?

Choosing the book	Making the calendar	Reading in class
Keeping a journal	Fishbowl discussions	Movie poster
Talk show	Vocabulary in context	

(Continued)

EXHIBIT 7.1 (Cont.)

COMPREHENSION ACTIVITIES

The groups engaged in several comprehension activities. As students began a book, I asked them to briefly write down what they thought the book was about from its title. I then asked them to read a few pages and answer these literature circles preview questions:

- After reading these pages, what do you think this book will be about?
- Pick a character introduced to you in these pages. Write the character's name and then describe this character and what you think of him or her.
- Write at least three questions you have about this book so far.
- What is your first impression of this book? Do you like it or dislike it? Why? Is it clear or confusing or funny or poetic? Explain your answer.

As they read, in addition to fishbowl discussions and work on learning vocabulary from context, students kept triple-entry, or action reading, journals. Each page of the journal had three columns. In the first column the student wrote a summary of the pages read that day and also a *golden line,* a line from the book that represented the theme of those pages. In the second column the student wrote one or more questions about what he or she had read. In the third column another student in the group wrote questions and opinions about the summary and the golden line and any answers he or she might have to the journal author's questions. This peer responder also signed his or her comments.

ASSESSMENT TOOLS

Even with all these strategies, it can be difficult to determine how well students comprehend a book (and sometimes even if they have read the book). I used multiple assessment tools to determine students' comprehension and reading behavior. In addition to completing the surveys, students wrote essays about general themes in their books. Also, in conjunction with an artist who worked in my classroom, the literature circles completed art projects that showed their knowledge of their book's theme. They could imagine that their book became a movie, and create a movie advertisement poster for it, or they could identify the book's theme, take photographs reflecting that theme, find a golden line in the book expressing that theme, and put all three elements together in a small poster.

Source: *Lisa Morehouse, based on literature circles from Harvey Daniels.*[1]

Another teacher introduces choice into her seventh-grade history classes by giving students three silent sustained reading (SSR) periods per week, during which they read self-selected texts related to the current history unit. She has focused a good deal of time and energy on developing her classroom library. In addition to borrowing books and other reading materials from the school library, she has been particularly persistent in finding extra money in her department and school for purchasing additional materials from local bookstores and thrift shops, building a library that has something for virtually everyone in her class. She has taken particular care to find reading matter that represents the various cultures of her students. As a result, when her students are studying the Middle Ages, they spend their SSR time reading everything from picture books with simple text about castles in France, Germany, or the greater Moorish empire to sophisticated fantasy novels set in medieval Europe or Asia. As students move through the year the books they choose are often longer, containing more information on topics of interest.

The Social Dimension: Making Problem Solving Visible and Safe

Many network participants working to develop reading apprenticeships with their students have found that teacher think-alouds serve two important purposes. In addition to making teachers' formerly invisible reading processes visible to students, the think-alouds make it safe for students to take risks in the classroom community. After all, if the teacher—the master reader—is willing to reveal his or her own confusion about a text, a student who feels confused won't feel so alone. More important, students will begin to see that confusion is a natural state of being for all readers at various points in their reading experience.

One eleventh-grade English teacher introduces the kind of problem-solving strategies needed to make sense of a difficult literary text by reading aloud the first paragraph of "Wash," a short story by William Faulkner. As he reads, he also thinks aloud about the text. Students are asked to categorize his think-alouds into five types of mental moves: picturing, questioning, summarizing, recalling, and clarifying. Similarly, a chemistry teacher thinks aloud as she demonstrates a laboratory procedure in front of her class, following instructions, making observations and careful descriptions, and drawing conclusions. These teachers draw students into the activity of consciously puzzling through texts and classroom activities. They begin the apprenticeship process by making thinking visible—and by making the confusions, false starts, and retracings that characterize reading for understanding an accepted part of classroom life.

One network teacher discovered a powerful way to build the social dimension of reading apprenticeship when she found she could not initiate literature discussions with her twelfth-grade literature class. Students were enrolled in the class because they did not have enough English units to graduate, and the class was boisterous and academically disinclined. However, the teacher noticed that one particular twelfth grader, athletic and attractive, held the attention of the entire class whenever he spoke. This young man also was among the least-skilled readers in the class. The teacher decided to put his popularity and attention seeking to good use, enlisting him in the role of facilitator for literature discussions. She capitalized on what he could do well, converse and lead his peers, to build social support for academic tasks that he could do less well.

As her students read *Brave New World*, she taught minilessons on thinking aloud and shared ways of asking good questions about literature. Students kept "think on paper" logs as they worked their way through the text. But the social interest generated by the popular young man asking questions about the text and facilitating conversation among students in the class was what really made the class work. Over time this teacher found that her students gained enough from class discussions that they could start to read parts of the text at home on their own, something these twelfth graders had never really done before.

The Cognitive Dimension: Developing Students' Mental Toolbelts

In closely considering their own reading processes, especially in dealing with discipline-specific texts, network teachers have come to appreciate the degree to which they rely on specific problem-solving strategies. With that in mind they make a point of sharing these strategies with their students, helping them build a mental toolbelt for problem solving when they read. As students begin using these strategies and, with enough guided practice, become increasingly independent in their reading, their teachers are able to dust off the class texts and bring them back into the curriculum.

One seventh-grade history and English teacher told us early in the year that she did not use the history textbook for a couple of reasons. For starters, she said, she could not rely on students to read the assignments. And when they did read the text, most of them seemed unable to summarize the ideas or put these ideas into their own words, leading her to believe they were not understanding what they read. She related, somewhat uncomfortably, that she found herself "spoon-feeding" the students, summarizing the key ideas *for* them. But as the year progressed and she found ways to help her students begin using comprehension strategies, she was able to reintroduce the course textbook with more confidence.

Questioning

Many network teachers find questioning a particularly powerful tool for making sense of texts. In particular, they find Taffy Raphael's question-answer relationships (described in Chapter Five) useful for helping students ask questions as they read and helping them understand the processes readers go through to answer different kinds of questions.

One tenth-grade humanities teacher teaches her students Raphael's four question types by using the room the class meets in as the subject of examples. A right there question such as "How many chairs are there?" is one the students can answer by merely looking. In contrast, a pulling it together question such as "Are the windows taller than the doors?" requires students to compare the relative sizes of the windows and the doors, looking back and forth and making mental approximations and calculations to answer.

After teaching the four question types in this way, the teacher moves to a novel the class is beginning. Students read a segment of the text and generate questions of each type, sharing and assessing their questions and the methods they use to answer them. Finally, pairs of students are assigned to generate two of each type of question for each chapter of the novel as they read. The pairs then take turns leading class discussions of the book based on the questions they have written. This teacher tells us she has been pleasantly surprised by the depth of her students' questions and the lively and engaged discussions they generate.

Network teachers have come up with a variety of ways to tie questioning strategies to the content curriculum and to projects that have meaning for the students. One teacher has her students create a test based on the question types to assess other students' understanding of an SSR book. Another has them design teaching units on their books, to be used by the English teachers at the school.

Summarizing

After joining the Strategic Literacy Network, the seventh-grade history and English teacher who had been summarizing the history textbook for her students decided to teach them to summarize the text on their own. Students worked in pairs, each pair focusing on a different section of the text. Each student wrote a summarizing sentence for the section and compared it with his or her partner's summary. The teacher was delighted to see the result: the student pairs combined or modified their sentences to create the best summary, working together to further clarify and actually negotiate the meaning of the section in order to write a summary that best encompassed the ideas in the text.

A teacher of sixth-grade English/language arts has her students generate a list of rules for a good summary. Working in groups, they write a summary of a story, such as a famous fairy tale that they all know well. Each group then reads its summary aloud, and the class rates the quality of the summary according to the rules. Next the teacher asks the groups of students to summarize a passage from a piece of literature they will be reading together as part of the curriculum. As they work to put the key events and ideas of the text into their own words, they continue to keep an eye on the criteria for a good summary.

A high school science teacher involves his marine science students in a similar process of generating the criteria for a good summary, creating and negotiating the content of a summary of a science article in small groups, and rating their own and other groups' summaries according to the criteria. He adds a few creative twists to this process, however: students must summarize all and only the key ideas of the science article in less than sixty words *and* in a poster that visually displays the key ideas. Summarizing with pictures stimulates the visual thinking that students must do to understand the physical processes of science.

Another science teacher, who teaches eleventh- and twelfth-grade conceptual chemistry, has found that students often have difficulty reading and following laboratory procedures. Of course the success of their lab work depends on accurate reading, and science students can become dependent on the teacher for constant review of instructions. To avoid constant requests to repeat directions, this teacher imposes an elaborate sense-making process on her students, making sure they have read and understood the directions before launching into a lab procedure (see Exhibit 7.2). Students work in groups to figure out what the procedure requires them to do. They then create a visual description of the process, using icons and symbols but "no complete sentences." When everyone in the group comprehends the procedure, the group goes to the teacher to retrieve the laboratory equipment. The teacher draws straws to see which student in the group she will test for understanding. The student can use only the group's pictorial description of the process as he or she describes the laboratory procedures. If the student passes the test, the group may proceed. If not, the group loses a point and is sent back to work to make sure the procedure is clear to all. Students quickly learn to make sense of lab procedures without relying on the teacher, and they become accustomed to using the picturing process to make sense of the text.

Imagining a Voice for the Text

In inquiries into their own reading processes, several network teachers have discovered that they use what they call a *voice-over* strategy to engage with text they find obscure, difficult, or simply uninteresting. They call up a voice—for example, the authoritative voice of a narrator on a nature documentary or of a news commentator—that they can imagine speaking in the style of the text at hand. They then imagine this voice reading the text.

EXHIBIT 7.2

Student Instructions for Labs

Cooperative Group Lab Format

Goal. For all group members to have a good understanding of the lab before starting the lab.

1. *Silently* read the entire lab procedure.
2. Discuss the procedure with your group. Be sure that you can answer the following questions.
    a. What is the overall point of the lab?
    b. What are the main procedures?
    c. What materials do you need for each procedure?
    d. What do you do in each procedure?
    e. Why do you do each step of the procedure?
3. Develop a visual that illustrates the lab procedure. (*Hint:* You need at least one picture for each main part of the lab.) Your visual can have labels, but no complete sentences are allowed. Be sure that you label lab equipment and all solutions.
4. Take turns explaining the procedure to each other using the visual. The group captain should go first. Make sure that you cover all of the important points. Use the chart below to evaluate each person's presentation. Feel free to practice several times to make sure that you are ready.

Name			
Understands overall point of the lab			
Includes all main procedures			
Includes materials			
Describes the procedures			
Explains the procedures			

5. When everyone in your group feels confident about his or her explanation, your whole group should bring its visual and come up to see me.
6. One person will be chosen at random to explain the procedure to me using the visual.
    a. If the explanation is satisfactory, your group may begin the lab. Set up your lab report as explained below, and get started on the lab.
    b. If the explanation is not satisfactory, your group will be sent back to repeat steps 4 through 6 until it is satisfactory. Your grade will be reduced each time that you are sent back (from an A to a B to a D). *You CANNOT start the lab until this is completed.*

Lab Report Format

Title	What is the name of the lab?
Purpose	What are you trying to find out?
Materials and procedure	Each person should copy the visual into his or her lab report once it has been satisfactorily completed.
Data	A data table clearly showing all of the data, with units for all measurements.
Calculations	Your calculations clearly shown, step-by-step. They should be labeled.

(Continued)

EXHIBIT 7.2 (Cont.)

Conclusion	Paragraph 1: Discuss the results of your experiment. What did you find out?
	Paragraph 2: How accurate do you think your results are? What could you do next time to get better results?
	Paragraph 3: What did you learn from this lab?
	Paragraph 4: Comment on the lab and the new lab format. What do you think of the new lab format? How did you like this lab? How well did you understand this lab compared to previous labs? Should I do this lab again next year?

Source: *Course materials created by Nicci Nunes.*

They say this strategy helps them gain better access to the ideas embedded in a difficult text.

A few network teachers teach this voice-over strategy to their students. One ninth-grade English teacher, for example, taught her culturally diverse students to approach standardized reading comprehension tests by imagining that they heard her voice—that of a teacher using standard English—reading the passage to them. Another ninth-grade humanities teacher teaches his students traditional comprehension strategies such as questioning and summarizing and adds to them what he calls the strategy of "imagining a voice for the author" as they read informational texts.

Evaluating and Choosing Workable Strategies

The goal of comprehension strategy instruction is for students to acquire mental tools that they can use as needed to assist their independent reading. Students' inquiries into their own reading processes should include ongoing evaluation of how well the various comprehension strategies are serving them. Subject area teachers can encourage students to choose strategies that work for them when reading independently.

For example, after engaging students in using various reading comprehension strategies during prior units, one ninth-grade English teacher started a new unit by giving students a set of *strategy sheets* (each sheet reviewing one strategy) and describing these familiar strategies as a kind of *strategy toolbox*. For this unit, students were to choose one of five different books to read and to make use of comprehension strategies independently or in small groups. For the first four days of the unit the teacher assigned a different comprehension strategy sheet every day, reminding students how they had used the particular comprehension strategy in prior units. After the first week the class discussed when and how each strategy was most useful. Throughout the rest of the unit the teacher asked students to choose one of the reading comprehension strategies from the strategy toolbox to use for each section of their chosen book. The only criterion the teacher gave them for making this choice was "choose the strategy you think will help you most to understand this reading." She found that different readers chose different strategies and that individual students chose different strategies to support their comprehension at different times.

The Knowledge-Building Dimension: Inviting Students into the Club

In considering how background knowledge contributes to effective reading, most network teachers focus first on building students' knowledge about content. But as teachers continue inquiring into their own reading, they begin to discover the depth and importance of their knowledge about the specialized conventions and vocabulary of disciplinary texts and about the particular ways one reads texts in different disciplines. At that point teachers begin to understand how demystifying the structures and conventions of disciplinary texts and teaching ways of reading them can increase students' access to disciplinary knowledge. Equally important, they begin to see how they can share this information with their students, helping them become part of the disciplinary *club*.

Building Knowledge About Content

A seventh-grade history teacher in the network has for some years tried to engage students with historical ideas and knowledge by having them work with a variety of materials including pictures, primary source documents, and some short expository pieces about the topic of study. She has had students use these materials in a variety of ways. They write journals from the perspective of someone living through the historical events portrayed. They write and role-play historical dramatizations based on the materials. They create a travel guide to another country, describing the dress, customs, food, religion, and system of government the traveler will encounter.

Now, to help her students become stronger readers of history, this teacher has begun to use these materials and projects in new ways. For example, she asks students to "read" the pictures that go along with the unit and "form some hypotheses" about what they see. Students talk with a partner, exchanging ideas about what the pictures might suggest about the culture, time period, or events they will be studying in the unit. Then students read the primary source documents or expository texts to confirm or refute their hypotheses, using a chart to keep track of what they think they know and what in the text triggers each idea. Through these activities, students collaboratively generate and extend their content ideas, thereby building a schema for the content they will encounter and preparing to read closely with this schema in mind.

This history teacher also helps her students build a framework for understanding a historical event they will read about by assigning them roles in the event and asking them to read and interpret a section of text or a primary source document from the perspective of that role. For example, if students read an account of an event as told by Cortés, they might then ask how Montezuma might have viewed that event. Yet another history teacher asks students to weigh the historical significance of what they will read, using the following criteria: (1) significant events and people are those that have the greatest impact, either positive or negative, on the lives of individuals and groups in a particular time period; (2) significant events and people are those that relate in some way to us in the present, who are affected by the past. This same teacher often asks students to take a position on a theme or issue that the class is studying, discuss their opinions with the class, and then read about a historical event in which the issue is raised. These prereading activities prepare students to read in a purposeful way, create a schema for the ideas they will encounter, and help them focus on what is important as they navigate through the text.

Similarly, a network science teacher presents laboratory experiments at the beginning of a unit to start building students' content schemata for particular scientific phenomena. Student observations during each experiment and the questions the experiment raises serve to both motivate and guide students through their subsequent reading of a textbook chapter. They read to discover the answers to authentic questions, and they read to understand and explain what they have observed in the experiment.

In the teaching of literature, teachers often incorporate a set of introductory activities designed to develop students' schemata in order to prepare them for the themes, relationships, and setting of a text. To bring students into the world of Anne Frank, for example, a teacher might begin reading Frank's diary by candlelight, telling her students in a hushed voice that if they are discovered they will be taken away to the Nazi death camps. In the novel *The Cay*, a black man and a white boy are adrift at sea and need to establish a relationship of trust in order to survive. One teacher introduced the setting and theme of *The Cay* to her sixth graders by drawing a raft-sized rectangle on the floor and assigning a boy and a girl to sit on the raft for the entire class period. She also asked students to empty their pockets and backpacks to see what, if anything, they had with them that might help them survive if they were to suddenly find themselves alone in unknown territory. How might they use these objects and their wits to feed, clothe, and shelter themselves?

Such prereading activities prime students for the ideas they will read about in a text, and even begin to build new content knowledge through collaborative sharing and elaboration of ideas. However, students are by and large recipients of these teacher-initiated, schema-building activities. To apprentice students to disciplinary reading, teachers must go further, helping students to call up and reflect on their own knowledge of a topic or situation and to generate their own ways to bring themselves into the world of a text. We return to these ideas later in this chapter.

Building Knowledge About Texts

Many network teachers have found that when students understand how a textbook is organized, they can more easily access information when they need it. A network science teacher has her students preview the textbook, working in groups to figure out how the text is structured and how its different elements function. Students read the title and subtitles, the illustrations and captions, and other information such as bold-faced words, the glossary, sidebar text, and guiding questions (see Exhibit 7.3). Such previews are intended to help them build a schema for the information they will read about and also a schema for the textbook's structure and organization. As a part of this same activity, students reflect on a recent textbook reading assignment, assessing how well they were able to do it. Then, on the basis of their group inquiry into the text structure, they make a plan for approaching such assignments in the future.

Teachers often think of graphic organizers as another way, using either pictures or a spatial arrangement of notes, to help students express their thoughts. Less often do they think of graphic organizers as tools to help students process the ideas and information in a text. One teacher told us, "When I've used graphic organizers before, it's been 'fluff work.' I never put that much emphasis on it because it was art work. I never really thought about what was going on in students' minds when they used them. But now I see that kids are using them as they work their way through the reading."

One seventh-grade history teacher in the network studied the kinds of text structures used in her course textbook. She found that as in most textbooks, each chapter used varied text structures, shifting unannounced from narrative to comparison and contrast to chronology to description. To

---

EXHIBIT 7.3

Student Instructions for Previewing a Text

Reading a Physics Textbook

What you do when you read a science textbook is very different from what you do when you read a novel or a history textbook. To be honest, everyone knows that a physics textbook isn't the most exciting reading. It is not meant to be. Instead it is meant to be a reference book to help you learn physics. In order for it to be useful to you, it is worth taking some time to look at the book. To do this, please follow the instructions below.

1. With your group look through chapter 4 of your physics textbook. Start from page 74 and turn the pages and write a list of all of the different types of things (sections, features, and so on) that you find in the chapter. Example: a picture above the title of the chapter.

2. Discuss your lists with the other groups in your team. Make additions to your list if you hear something that you missed.

3. After the discussion, read through your list again with your group, and for each part discuss and answer the following questions: Why is this part included in the book? What is it useful for? Example: the picture at the beginning of the chapter is put there to try to interest the reader in the subject as well as give the reader an idea of what he or she will be learning in this chapter.

4. Recently, I gave you a couple of reading assignments. First, I asked you to read sections 4-1 through 4-3 and to answer some questions. Did you do the assignment? If not, why not? If you did, how did you go about it? Was there anything about the way the book is organized and presented that helped you?

5. In the second reading assignment, I asked you to read section 4-4 and to look at the example problems. Did you do the assignment? If not, why not? If you did, how did you go about it? Was there anything about the way the book is organized and presented that helped you?

6. Thinking about everything that you have discussed today, make a list of the types of things that you think people should do when they are reading a physics textbook to help them best understand the material. Example: Whenever you see an equation, you should write it on your notecard and make sure that you know what each symbol stands for and what the equation is used for.

7. Looking at your list from step 6, which techniques will you try when you read sections 4-5 and 4-6? Why did you pick those techniques?

8. What did you learn from looking at the textbook? Was it useful? Do you think it will help you read the textbook? Do you think it will help you learn physics better?

Source: *Course materials created by Nicci Nunes.*

---

help demystify these shifts in text structure, she slightly revised the signal words and phrases list that we used in the Academic Literacy course (Exhibit 5.1), and then provided a graphic organizer for each kind of text structure, which students could use in their note taking (Exhibit 7.4).

Students used this list to figure out what type of text they were reading. As a class they also generated and posted around the classroom a set of *traffic signs* to go along with each signal word. For example, the words *but* and *however* were represented with a stop sign and a U-turn sign together, meaning readers should stop and go the other way. The process

EXHIBIT 7.4

Graphic Organizers for Text Structures

If You Read …	You Might Expect to Find …	You Can Probably Use This Note-Taking Strategy
1. A question	1. An answer, or the information to create an answer	*Question:* _____ •*Information* •*Answer* *Answer:* _____
2. Colon (:)	2. A list	*Main Idea:* •*Detail* •*Detail* •*Detail*
3. Therefore	3. Results or conclusions	*This is* — *Because* ◯ / *Because* ◯
4. That is (i.e.) In other words Consists of Is equal to Means	4. A definition	*Highlight* •*Term* •*Key terms* •*Definition* *Term* *Definition/Sentence*
5. For example (e.g.) For instance Such as Is like Including To illustrate	5. Examples	*Main Idea* *Ex 1* *Ex 2* *Ex 3* *or* *Main Idea* •*Example* •*Example*
6. Similarly In the same way Just like Just as Likewise In comparison Also	6. Comparison (how things are similar or the same)	*A* / *A+B* / *B* ; *A* *A* / *A* *A+B* *B*
7. In contrast On the other hand However Whereas But Yet	7. Contrast (how things are different)	*A* / *A+B* / *B* ; *A* | *B*
8. This caused An effect of Because of In response to As a result of	8. A cause-and-effect relationship, or how something happened	*A*) *Led to* / *B*) *Led to* / *C* ; *A* → *B* → *C* → *D* *All caused*
9. Before Preceding Prior to Previously During Concurrently Following After	9. A sequence of events, timeline, or chronology	*Before* *During* *After*

of generating these signs for tracking the moves of a nonfiction text was probably as helpful for students as were the completed and posted signs.

This teacher also aligned note-taking assignments with the text structures her students were encountering at the time. For example, when reading a narrative about the life of Mohammed, students were expected to write journal notes in a narrative chronology. When reading a comparison between the lives of a serf and a nobleman in feudal Europe, students were asked to include a Venn diagram in their notes. Over time, students learned to choose an appropriate graphic organizer and note-taking system on their own, based on the signal words and structure they saw in the text. In reading apprenticeship classrooms, teachers can show students how to read the clues to text structure that are available in a text and to select a graphic organizer to support their reading.

Network English teachers, like their colleagues in social studies, have found ways to help their students read *text moves.* They let students know that even experienced readers of literature are often confused at the start of the piece of fiction but that they have various ways of orienting themselves as they continue reading. Absent this understanding, many students, especially those who do not think of themselves as readers to begin with, attribute their confusion to poor reading skills, assuming that everyone else magically understands the literature right away. The network literature teachers decided to introduce this idea to students through silent films and films with the sound turned off. After showing a few moments from the beginning of a film, the teachers pause it and ask students what they know or can guess about the story so far. Who is the main character? Where is this film taking place? When? What is going to happen? What clues are students using to draw these conclusions? Students discover that they identify these clues in part through their knowledge of the conventions of particular film genres. They know that comedies, mysteries, dramas, and action adventures each tend to have particular kinds of characters and plots. The teachers then point out that the same is true of different types of literature.

Many contemporary novels freely and regularly shift point of view, settings, and time periods. A narrative might for example shift from internal monologue to conversation to description of past or current events. These shifts are among the aspects of literature that are most mystifying to students. Several teachers address students' confusion by explicitly drawing their attention to shifts in voice, time, perspective, and setting. They ask students to notice how they can tell when such shifts occur. What is it about the text that marks the shifts? What are the clues? This type of conversation demystifies this common characteristic of contemporary fiction, helping students read more like proficient readers of literature.

Just as students can be unaware of and therefore frustrated by an author's sudden shifts of voice or time frame in a text, they can be confused and sometimes defeated by the different styles of language and tone that appear across pieces of literature. We have seen students who can work effectively with texts like Terry McMillan's *Mama* and Shakespeare's *Romeo and Juliet* but are completely unable to enter James Thurber's world of caustic wit and irony. One English teacher addresses this issue by having students work in groups to excerpt short, descriptive phrases and record all the information these descriptions give about setting and character development. Students work collaboratively to demystify the use of figurative language, an approach that helps identify the types of textual clues that readers can use to discern meaning. One ninth grader explained how she knew when a word was being used figuratively in an excerpt from Solzhenitsyn's *Gulag Archipelago:* "We weren't talking about a machine, but all of a sudden here's the word 'machine,' so I knew it couldn't really mean machine. It had to mean something else."

Network teachers also use popular culture to help students think through the interpretive thinking they employ to understand popular song lyrics. Teachers then draw parallels to the ways experienced readers approach fiction. One ninth-grade English teacher begins a poetry unit by introducing her students to the importance of reading on various interpretive levels. She starts with the words from slave spirituals such as "The Drinking Gourd" and "Swing Low, Sweet Chariot." She has students imagine themselves as slaves, finding coded ways to communicate escape plans to one another under the very eyes and ears of the slave owners. When the spiritual advises the weary slave to "follow the drinking gourd" to the river where "the old man is a-waiting for to carry you to freedom," students begin to see the double meanings hidden in the song. Through activities like these, students can discover and share how they already make meaning on different levels as they view films, interpret popular culture and conversations, and read literature. They become more conscious that words mean different things on different interpretive and figurative levels. How does a person know, for example, when something is a joke? When someone is speaking sarcastically? When someone isn't serious?

Building Knowledge About Disciplinary Ways of Reading

To support their students in becoming stronger readers of a broader range of disciplinary texts, Strategic Literacy Network teachers continue working to identify the knowledge and ways of reading they themselves bring to various texts. Ways of reading and thinking are often linked. Reading in science, for example, can be a search for information and truth, much like the discipline itself. Reading in history invokes a more interpretive frame.

In their inquiries into science reading, teachers noticed a distinctive difference between the way experienced readers of literature read words and the way experienced science readers read words. Literature readers have a great deal of tolerance for multiple meanings because in fiction and poetry the significance of words often extends beyond any literal definition. Words may have literal, figurative, and symbolic meanings all at once. In science, by contrast, proficient readers narrow in on precise definitions of key words. For example, a word like *friction* conveys a concept that has been the subject of experimentation, observation, and discovery for centuries, and its meaning has changed over time as scientists learned more about and more precisely articulated the underlying scientific phenomena.

Network science teachers have also realized that in reading a scientific piece, they are reading to dispel any naïve ideas they may have held about how particular scientific phenomena work. They saw, for example, that in reading an article describing classical ideas about friction and key experiments that had uncovered its real properties, their lay definition of this word was displaced by the more precise, scientific definition given in the article. Realizing that as they read science, they often rejected old definitions in favor of more precise and up-to-date definitions, teachers concluded that their common practice of giving students definitions of key words before reading a science text was misguided. They decided, instead, to have students use a graphic organizer to explore the definitions and examples they had in mind for key scientific concepts *before* reading the text and then to track how the discoveries and experiments discussed in the text changed their definitions of these words *as they read*. In this way, science teachers were showing their students how to read and think like scientists.

Because the network now includes teachers of science and history as well as literature, members have become more attuned to the fact that different disciplines tend to engender or require different reading styles. In reading literature and historical essays with other teachers in the network, one high school history teacher noticed that though she reads nonfiction keenly, she has very little patience for the language play and aesthetics of literature. Learning that she reads differently than other teachers in the network has made her aware of different reading styles and bents among her students and has motivated her to find ways to demystify nonfiction reading for student readers who have a literary bias.

After reading a difficult expository piece in science, one high school literature teacher said that being put in a situation where she was reading at what she called her "frustration" level gave her more empathy for her students and reminded her that she needed to be more diplomatic and collegial with the teachers in other departments at her school. There are ways of reading that students need to acquire in the subject areas, expert ways of navigating through texts and thinking in the ways literary or scientific or historical thinkers think. Network teachers have come to see that these ways with words can be taught and learned.

Embedding Reading Apprenticeship: Where to Begin?

It is one thing to learn about many reading strategies designed to support student reading in subject areas and something else again to start incorporating these strategies into regular classroom practice. Teachers' common question is, Where do I start?

Becoming aware of your own reading processes is the essential first step in helping students focus on how they read and, therefore, on their ongoing development as successful discipline-specific readers. As you read, on your own and with your students, two questions must be in the forefront of your mind: How did I come to my understanding of what this text may mean? What is invisible here that I need to make visible for my students?

Ask your students to begin talking and writing about their own reading processes, about how they read and make sense of texts. Begin to build their metacognitive awareness as they read. Create the metacognitive conversation.

We recommend that when teachers begin embedding reading strategies in their subject area classrooms, they

- Keep it simple, choosing just one or two key strategies or activities for supporting students' reading in the discipline.

- Weave these strategies into the classroom curricular routine.

- Adopt a cycle of repeatedly experimenting with, reassessing, and then refining the use of these key strategies.

- Move students toward independence, helping them become increasingly autonomous in using the strategies and gradually curtailing direct teacher involvement and support.

In the next chapter we describe some of the issues and challenges teachers encounter as they work to support students' reading and invite you to further explore these issues with us.

Notes

1. H. Daniels, *Literature Circles: Voice and Choice in the Student-Centered Classroom* (York, M.E.: Stenhouse Publications, 1994).

Chapter 8

Overcoming Obstacles in Implementation

ALTHOUGH WE KNOW that reading apprenticeships can help students from the least skilled to the most skilled, we also know that teachers must consider the particular needs of individual students in order to fully support these students as developing readers. The reading apprenticeship approach we have described in the prior chapters arose in collaboration among many committed and thoughtful teachers. In this chapter we comment on some of the broad challenges that teachers have encountered in implementing reading apprenticeships. We invite you to collaborate with us in finding new ways to meet these long-standing challenges.

Different Students, Different Needs

It is a common assumption that students who are poor readers are also poor thinkers. Because reading apprenticeships rely on students' metacognitive and strategic thinking and aim to put students in control of their reading processes, educators sometimes wonder if this approach can help their lowest-skilled students. In our experience, however, the students who score lowest on the Degrees of Reading Power test we administer at the beginning of the year make the greatest gains through the reading apprenticeship approach.

One English as a second language teacher who has participated in the Strategic Literacy Network for two years said the students in her transition-level English as a second language (ESL) class had all been born in the United States and had gone through the U.S. educational system. Nonetheless, in eighth grade these students were still in a transitional ESL class, were unmotivated, and as their teacher put it, had come to identify themselves as low achievers. Yet between October and May of one school year, seventeen of these twenty students had increased their standardized test scores by more than 20 points (2 points is a normal year's growth in reading at the secondary level, according to the test designers).

If reading apprenticeship works well for students who have been low performers in the past, what about high performers? Some educators have questioned whether their more successful readers have anything to gain from the kind of instructional support outlined in this book. But those in our network who teach honors and college preparation classes are often discouraged by their students' reliance on Cliff Notes and other reading aids and by how little these students read beyond their school assignments. Moreover, in our collegial inquiries into reading, teachers themselves often recall having struggled through their first years of college as they learned on their own how to read difficult academic texts. This is all to say that even the so-called best readers have much to gain from developing insight into their own sense-making processes and from gaining knowledge about the structures and conventions of particular texts. This is especially true in this age of burgeoning information, when new and unfamiliar texts will be a part of students' futures as readers.

Building Fluency for the Lowest-Skilled Readers

Given enough time, the vast majority of secondary students can decode words, even multisyllabic words. Most often the lowest-skilled readers are held back not by an inability to decode but by a lack of fluency in decoding; that is, their decoding is not automatic. They must focus so hard on pronouncing the words that they tend to lose focus on comprehension. A great deal of research has shown that students gain fluency by reading extensively in texts that are at their independent reading level—texts they can read with 95 percent comprehension, as measured by comprehension questions about the text.[1] At this level, students may encounter challenging words but they do so at a low frequency, so the process of expanding their reading vocabulary does not disrupt their comprehension. Instead, their comprehension can assist them to figure out what the unfamiliar words are likely to mean. This is how both vocabulary and reading proficiency grow through reading.

In Chapter Four we described the role of silent sustained reading (SSR) in reengaging adolescents with books and in giving them opportunities for increasing their fluency and stamina as readers. However, some of the least-proficient readers may need activities in addition to SSR and extra support to develop into fluent readers. In addition, a major obstacle to building fluency for poor adolescent readers is the stigma they feel when they can read only what they consider baby books with ease. Reducing or eliminating this stigma is key to helping them.

An ingenious and successful way to mitigate the stigma of poor reading is reported in *Buddy Reading*.[2] The authors, Katherine Samway, Gail Whang, and Mary Pippitt, created a program in which very low-skilled fifth-grade readers became reading partners for second-grade readers. To prepare, the fifth graders were required to read an enormous quantity of young children's literature so they would be able to recommend titles to their second-grade buddies. They kept logs with summaries of the books, new vocabulary words, and comprehension questions to ask their buddies. This study and preparation for the weekly reading sessions with their partners was just what the fifth graders needed to develop fluency and confidence as readers. Moreover, they were motivated to work hard by being identified as "more skilled" readers who, for once in their school careers, had something to share.

Clearly this program took a great deal of teacher organization and oversight as well as resources in the form of young children's fiction and nonfiction texts. When the goal is to develop the fluency and skill of poor readers, it is not enough simply to assign them to read once a week to young readers. The coordination between teachers and sometimes between schools will take someone's time, interest, and commitment, but it can be done.

Research points educators to a variety of other ways to help students develop fluency, but if these methods are to work with adolescents, each will take the kind of ingenuity the Buddy Reading program demonstrates. Repeated readings of texts that are slightly above students' comfort levels form one proven way to address fluency problems.[3] But how can one get adolescents to read the same, slightly challenging text repeatedly?

We can imagine assigning adolescent students to create books on tape for younger readers, for libraries, for the blind, for seniors, or for prisoners. Students can pick texts that motivate them and that they believe their audiences will love, then practice reading orally with expression, taping and retaping their efforts until they have a complete text. These could be novel-length works or short stories, dramas or informational texts. Again, a successful program of books on tape would require coordination, organization, and resources.

Another well-known approach to building fluency is choral reading and its variant, readers theater. We can imagine engaging a group of adolescents in practicing fluent oral reading with assigned parts for a performance of some kind. An antismoking campaign or a plea for tolerance of differences among the teenagers in a school, for example, might be a cause the reading could address. It is very important to consider the variety of texts one wants students to read fluently, so performances across the curriculum might include informational texts as well as poetry, drama, and fiction.

Of course when students practice fluency through oral reading they must understand what they are reading aloud, not just pronounce the words without comprehension. Readers theater is a good venue for building both fluency and comprehension because the reader or group of readers must decide what a passage means before they can give the words the proper emphasis and interpretation for the audience. Because poor readers often equate reading with pronouncing words well, however, bringing comprehension to the forefront in these activities will require vigilance from innovating classroom teachers.

When Decoding Is Still a Problem

As we noted earlier, even though they may lack fluency, the vast majority of students are able to decode by the time they reach secondary school. Those who are not yet comfortable with decoding may have language or learning problems. Identifying the difficulties underlying decoding problems and then the best instructional approaches for students with these difficulties is a task best addressed by reading specialists and expert educational testing. Often those few students who do have difficulty decoding at the secondary level have already been identified as resource or special education students. As such, they are qualified for special services. If a teacher suspects a student who has not been so identified of having decoding difficulties, the student should be referred for testing and evaluation.

When additional support is needed for such a student or group of students, resources are usually available from a reading specialist at the school or from resource teachers in the school's Special Education Department. These students may also benefit from school volunteers and tutoring services. The best support services we have seen have been provided to students, their teachers, and their peers during class time, not in special pull-out programs. We have also seen school administrators provide subject area teachers with time for coordinating with special education staff. Some particularly innovative approaches to team teaching place special education staff inside the classroom to support all students having difficulty, not just those with identified learning differences.

In our network of secondary teachers, we have worked with several resource teachers who have found reading apprenticeships useful in their work with special education students. Instructional approaches such as thinking aloud, using cognitive strategies while reading, and identifying the structures of texts have helped these students understand the hidden comprehension processes that support reading. These resource teachers have also found ways to simplify and support comprehension strategy use that other network teachers have found invaluable. Not incidently, resource teachers often gather libraries of books that link with the content curriculum, concern topics of interest to a variety of students, and are written at various levels.

In other words, special education and resource teachers can be a tremendous source of information, texts, and reading approaches that work for students having difficulty. They are often familiar with a variety of approaches to reading that build on the particular strengths (and sidestep the particular weaknesses) of individual students. For example, chunking words into larger, common patterns consisting of *onsets* (consonants or consonant clusters) and *rimes* (vowels plus ending sounds) is a technique familiar to many resource teachers that can assist students who cannot segment and sequence independent sounds to decode more efficiently.

The challenge for the classroom teacher—and the school administrator—is to coordinate all the relevant resources at the school—including materials, specialized personnel, volunteers, and tutors—well enough to routinely provide extra support to the students who need it, when they need it.

Reading and the Second Language Learner

Often teachers assume that students who are learning English as a second language must develop their oral English before they will be able to benefit from reading. Sheltered approaches to subject area teaching and multimodal approaches to teaching key concepts and vocabulary are highly beneficial to these and many other students. However, reading itself also helps build English language proficiency for ESL learners.

Through reading apprenticeships, teachers engage students in inquiry into their own reading processes, their likes, and their dislikes and give them strategies for making sense of texts as independent readers. They work to demystify the structure of texts and identify the language features characteristic of particular kinds of texts. These are precisely the kinds of approaches that have been found to assist second language learners in becoming more skillful and confident readers of English.

ESL learners benefit not only from strategic reading instruction but also from extensive and broad reading. Extensive reading on a particular topic builds background knowledge and specific vocabulary, including semantically related words. For example, when students read two or three passages from different sources on the same topic, they encounter a similar but not exact match of words and ideas, and they can draw on what they already know about the topic as they expand their knowledge by this further reading. Similarly, broad reading of a variety of genres helps ESL learners understand the different ways English works in different texts.

As teachers and administrators know, immigrant students arrive in U.S. schools at all grade levels and with all kinds of previous educational and literacy experiences and knowledge. Providing texts that answer their varied needs is a challenging, but necessary task. Appropriate materials are essential. ESL teachers need extensive classroom libraries with high-interest, easy-reading texts of all kinds. Schools and departments need to collect multiple texts at various levels on topics that are central to the curriculum in order to help ESL learners develop the background knowledge and vocabulary they need to access the curriculum. Given sufficient organization and support, a reading program for ESL learners can contribute to oral language development and subject area learning just as these achievements can feed back into students' reading.

Cultural Values Related to Reading and Achievement

Adolescents seek to belong—to identify themselves with others. Unfortunately, they often value the opinions of others who do not value reading, and in order to belong, they too seek identities as nonreaders. In the Academic Literacy course we worked hard to find authors who would give young people from different cultural and ethnic groups permission to achieve as readers. For instance, we found Malcolm X, Frederick Douglass, and Claude Brown to be valuable allies in the challenge of engaging young African American men with reading. In a similar vein, a teacher who had just moved from an urban area to the rural Midwest asked us for a list of equally compelling authors for white, rural young men who do not see reading as part of their future.

Educators teach a variety of students who identify themselves in a variety of ways but often in opposition or resistance to reading. Sometimes these identities are shaped around ethnicity; often they are not. There are the skateboarders, the bike tricksters, the socialites who plan school events, the jocks, the musicians.

One way we have tried to work with the adolescent need for identity formation, for experimentation around identity, and for self-confidence during an overwhelmingly disconcerting time of life is by engaging young people in inquiry. Asking questions about the role reading will play in their futures gives students permission to set and reevaluate their own goals and the pathways they might take to reach them. We are now considering establishing a youth advisory board to the Strategic Literacy Initiative. Drawing on young people's orientation to service, we would ask board members to carry out real research into the ways their peers read and interpret a variety of texts, from popular culture media to the texts required in different workplaces. These adolescents might also serve as *literacy advocates* or *ambassadors,* speaking powerfully to other young people about the importance of reading for self and society. We know that classroom reading apprenticeships rely on both the willing engagement of the apprentice and access to his or her reading experiences. A youth advisory board could help us learn how to better mine the untapped resources of adolescents. We can imagine a similar youth advisory approach working in a classroom or a school.

Challenges for Subject Area Teachers

When subject area teachers think about embedding a reading apprenticeship approach in their classes they foresee a deep tension arising between the ever-present pressure to cover the curriculum and the goal of helping students become independent readers and learners. As we observed in Chapter One, student reading difficulties can look so daunting that teachers opt to teach around the texts to ensure that students have access to the curriculum. But in our experience, when teachers make the commitment to help students with reading and spend time in the beginning of the year establishing comprehension rituals that support students and lead to increased independent reading throughout the year, this initial investment does not necessarily displace content coverage.

One network history teacher, whose students initially could not summarize the texts they read or put a text's ideas into their own words, spent time at the beginning of the year teaching a single comprehension strategy. She had students work in pairs to summarize chunks of the text and then evaluate and revise their summaries. She found that by thus wrestling with the texts, her students began focusing more on the deep ideas of the curriculum and that the activity did not take much class time away from content teaching. Instead, this work supported the content.

We would not want to claim, however, that there are no trade-offs between teaching students the content of the curriculum and teaching them processes for accessing content through reading. Each teacher ultimately weighs these options and strikes a balance, often reconciling himself or herself to a compromise of some kind.

Reading Extensively in Subject Area Classes

Given the demanding curricula of many subject area classes, teachers may have difficulty reconciling the need for extensive reading to build text knowledge and fluency with the need to cover important topics. Extensive reading, which provides many benefits to students, must be carefully linked to the curriculum for teachers to justify using precious class time for it.

Extensive reading on one topic builds background knowledge and vocabulary not only for second language learners but for all readers. One way of offering students this opportunity is to provide them with multiple source texts on a particular topic of study as often as possible. Texts might be taken from older textbooks that are no longer in use or from the primary source documents supplied in textbooks. Modern textbooks often offer excerpts from a variety of sources, providing multiple perspectives on historical events. Reading these different sources also gives students the opportunity to encounter specific vocabulary and ideas from multiple perspectives. Similarly, students can encounter specific vocabulary and ideas in multiple ways by reading an old textbook version of a historical event alongside the version in a newer textbook. Often they will find that historical events are presented from different perspectives in the two textbooks.

Students will need help accessing these materials. They will also need encouragement to see reading of multiple texts as a worthwhile investment of their time. You may want to have them keep a log comparing the two or three texts to one another. Is one easier to understand? More interesting? What makes it so? You may also want to help students reflect on what they know about a topic before reading, what they learn from reading a first text on the topic, and what they learn from reading another text on the same topic. This reflection may help them recognize that their understanding grows the more they read on a topic.

Silent sustained reading has not traditionally been a part of subject area classrooms, but this is another way to provide students with multiple texts and extensive reading opportunities. If teachers have classroom libraries with a variety of texts linked to curriculum topics, SSR can become part of a science class, a history class, or even an art or shop or government class. Internet Web pages and current newspaper or magazine articles on science, technology, government, or foreign affairs offer texts that can be linked to curriculum units and brought into the classroom for students to choose from.

Many subject area teachers use particular activities at the start of the class period to quiet students after the passing period and focus them on the topics of study. SSR can become one of these regular activities.

Students can choose texts that interest them and read for ten to fifteen minutes on two or three days a week. To the extent that these texts are linked to curriculum units, students are learning the content while also reading more widely and extensively in the subject area. To link the reading even more explicitly to the curriculum, teachers might ask students to keep reading logs that address particular questions or might occasionally facilitate conversations about what the students are learning during the SSR.

Test Pressures

Test pressures are simply a variation of the pressures to cover certain content. Increasingly, schools and teachers are being held accountable for student performance on standardized tests of reading and discipline-based knowledge. Teachers often feel they face a choice in which no one wins: derail the curriculum and teaching practices they know to be effective in order to prepare for the test or resist test pressures and hope for the best in terms of their students' performances on these exams. There is, however, another choice, one that is in the spirit of the apprenticeship model laid out in this book.

Teachers can think of these tests as a unique genre: texts constructed for particular purposes with particular formats and uses of language and reflecting genre-specific ways of thinking. They can work with their students to demystify the purposes, formats, and expected responses of these tests. By doing student and teacher think-alouds, employing a variety of cognitive strategies, and sharing reading processes in this particular reading situation, they can begin to share and build on each other's strengths and experiences as test takers. Lucy Calkins and colleagues, for example, describe a curriculum in which teachers and students take this approach, demystifying the genre of standardized tests.[4]

Standardized tests in history, mathematics, and science ask students to demonstrate mastery over a particular body of knowledge and the ability to comprehend discipline-based texts. We would argue that a reading apprenticeship approach in a subject matter class helps students access and more deeply process the content of the discipline and therefore prepares them to retain more of the knowledge tested.

Addressing the Challenges

We began this chapter acknowledging the teachers whose work is making headway toward overcoming some of the obstacles to implementation discussed here. We would like to continue to learn from teachers working to address these challenges.

Specifically,

- We'd like to collect and share more examples of ways teachers are working, especially in their content areas, to build fluency for adolescents.

- We'd like to know about other successful models for providing the kind of extra reading support some students need.

- We'd like to learn about more ways in which educators are successfully working with young people to help them develop identities as readers. Who are the young people you have trouble reaching? Who are the authors that can speak to them about the value of academic achievement, in general, and reading in particular?

- Given this time of tight budgets and public skepticism, we'd like to collect and share with other educators some of the ways teachers are managing to get the resources they need to help all students access a variety of texts.

- We'd also like to learn from subject area teachers who manage to set time aside for reading ancillary materials despite the pressure to cover so much curriculum.

- We'd like to consider, with others, how departments, school communities, and policymakers outside of schools can make decisions about what kind of balance we want to strike between content "coverage" needs and the need to build students' comprehension capabilities.

- Finally, we'd like to hear about other related issues and challenges we have yet to recognize or to face. In the Epilogue we invite readers to join an ongoing conversation though our Web site [www.wested.org/stratlit].

Notes

1. C. Snow, S. Burns, and P. Griffin, *Preventing Reading Difficulties in Young Children* (National Reading Academy Press, 1998); S. J. Samuels, "The Method of Repeated Readings," *The Reading Teacher,* Feb. 1997, *50*(5), 376–381; D. R. Reutzel and R. B. Cooler Jr., *Balanced Reading Strategies and Practices: Assisting and Assessing Readers with Special Needs* (Columbus, Ohio: Merrill, 1999); R. R. Day and J. Bamford, *Extensive Reading in the Second Language Classroom* (Cambridge University Press, 1998).

2. K. D. Samway, G. Whang, and M. Pippitt, *Buddy Reading: Cross-Age Tutoring in a Multicultural School* (Portsmouth, N.H.: Heinemann, 1995).

3. S. J. Samuels, "The Method of Repeated Readings."

4. L. Calkins, K. Montgomery, and D. Santman, *A Teacher's Guide to Standardized Reading Tests: Knowledge Is Power* (Portsmouth, N.H.: Heinemann, 1998).

Part Three

Beyond the Classroom

Chapter 9

Professional Development: Creating Communities of Master Readers

AS IN ANY APPRENTICESHIP, in a reading apprenticeship success depends in large part on how well the master understands and can articulate and demonstrate his or her craft, in this case, making sense of text. Because most proficient readers, teachers included, read in a fairly automatic fashion, the first step in becoming a master reader is to start paying attention in a new way to how one reads. Teachers must become explicitly aware of how they tackle challenging text in general and text within their own disciplines in particular.

Demystifying their own reading processes helps middle and high school subject area teachers work with knowledge and authority in a domain they have often seen as belonging to others—to reading experts, resource teachers, or researchers. The average middle or secondary school subject area teacher does not think of himself or herself as a reading teacher and does not feel qualified to help students with reading. But our own experience with the Strategic Literacy Network has shown us that subject area teachers who tune in to their own reading processes begin to see their roles differently and become more confident about what they have to offer in supporting student reading. As one teacher said, "The process of looking closely at my own reading enabled me to begin to demystify reading for my students."

Network teachers and researchers read together regularly, articulating, analyzing, and sharing the ways each goes about solving various reading problems. Through such collegial inquiry, these subject area teachers come to see that as successful readers in their own disciplines, they are their own best resources and guides in helping students learn how to master the texts related to those disciplines. They realize that in addition to a broad repertoire of comprehension strategies they can employ with difficult texts, they possess substantial knowledge about the *codes* of their respective disciplines. Among these codes are idiosyncratic vocabulary and usage patterns, historical and contextual references, and conventional ways of thinking, all of which are reflected in any discipline's texts. Teachers begin to see that by teaching these strategies and codes in the natural course of a subject area class, they are helping students develop independent access to the substance of a discipline.

Through collegial inquiry, network teachers also learn or are reminded that just as a single proficient reader does not approach all texts in exactly the same way, different proficient readers will approach the same text in varied ways. As these teachers continue to read together, they expand their own repertoires of comprehension strategies and knowledge about how to read effectively within and across disciplines.

With a growing understanding of their own reading processes and of the fact that there is no one right way to approach all the different kinds of texts, teachers become ready to begin their work as master readers. At this point they can begin to transform their classrooms into communities of inquiry in which students and teacher together explore content and, as a way of accessing that content, general and discipline-specific reading processes.

Learning How Versus Being Told

The difference between *being told* how something works and *learning how* something works from one's own experience is considerable. Most professional development related to secondary school reading is closest to the being told variety of development. An outside reading expert typically provides a rundown of key comprehension strategies, such as "find the main idea," "make predictions," "question the text," and "summarize." Some subject area teachers then turn around and deliver these strategies to their students in much the same way, in the form of instructional add-ons to their content curriculum. More often they find teaching these strategies burdensome and easily sacrificed in the press to cover more of the core curriculum.

Being told that a strategy like "predicting by using chapter headings and subheadings" can help one make sense of texts may have some usefulness. But that usefulness will not compare to knowing how to sort through, choose, and orchestrate the multiple strategies generally required to make sense of complex or unfamiliar text. Reading comprehension problems may be of similar types but in their details they often differ substantially, and more powerful by far than learning a set of disconnected reading comprehension strategies is the experience of sitting down and working through real comprehension problems in real texts with other readers. Rather than a burdensome instructional add-on, practice in reading strategically in the texts of a discipline can be central to learning subject area knowledge. And secondary teachers already know how to work through comprehension problems in a disciplinary text; in their own content-based reading they do it all the time, albeit most often unconsciously.

Inquiry-based professional development helps teachers tap into and further develop that know-how. Looking hard at one's own reading processes and at the same time inquiring into the reading of others, whether colleagues, research partners, or students, yields a deeper and more integrated knowledge of how people make sense of text. That growing knowledge enables a subject area teacher to develop a classroom language for talking about reading, to better understand what a student's comments might convey about his or her reading process, and to create new and different learning opportunities around subject area materials and curriculum.

Knowing how they solve their own reading comprehension problems also gives teachers a powerful point of view from which to judge the appropriateness of various teaching approaches. We believe teachers who engage in reading inquiry are well prepared to deal with the shifting and often contradictory advice that comes from those billed as experts. In the recent resurgence of the reading wars, for example, both code-based and literature-based approaches to reading instruction have been either embraced or attacked wholesale in public discourse. Classroom teachers who see themselves not as master readers but merely as reading trainees or recipients of others' expertise are most vulnerable to such dizzying swings of the public opinion and policy pendulum.

Exploring Reading as Colleagues

Developing an explicit awareness of one's own reading process is more challenging and complex than one might expect. Although research tells us that the reader of this or any other text is coordinating multiple interpretive strategies to make sense of it, readers normally use and orchestrate such strategies without conscious awareness, intent, or effort. Making one's own reading explicit involves focusing on complex mental processes that most teachers use unconsciously; it is sort of like trying to understand how one walks. To serve as master readers, teachers need to bring to the surface what most often goes on under the surface.

Although an individual teacher can certainly reflect on his or her reading processes, especially through a reading journal, we have found that teachers derive greater benefit from analyzing their craft in a community of other master readers. Our experiences with the Strategic Literacy Network have shown us that teachers can help each other overcome some of the natural awkwardness of trying to focus on one's own reading processes. Equally important, in a group teachers discover that others' reading processes do not necessarily mirror their own.

For all of us, sharing our thinking with others can actually help us pay closer attention to things that may otherwise go unnoticed. Hearing another reader explain something he or she did to make sense of a text may well trigger a realization that we did something quite similar—or, conversely, something quite different—even though we were not tuned in to our strategy at the time. In a similar vein, teachers who explore reading in a community of colleagues begin to see that all readers have a repertoire of strategies and stores of knowledge that serve them well for some texts and less well for others. They also experience firsthand that all readers can be defeated by some texts. When these understandings inform their work, teachers are more likely to offer students a broad repertoire of strategies and ways of reading rather than expecting that one approach will suit all readers and reading situations. As one teacher said, "I thought I was aware of what I do when I read. This was not necessarily the case. As I became more aware of what good readers do as they read, I found this understanding creeping more and more into my teaching. And of course the more the kids became aware of the reading processes, the more content they could draw from text."

Activities for Analyzing Reading Processes

In our work with middle and high school teachers, we have developed some reading inquiry activities that have helped readers—ourselves included—become more aware of their own reading processes. We offer four of them here as examples of inquiry-based professional development that we have found particularly powerful in helping subject area teachers gain the skill and the will to assist students with reading classroom texts. We urge teachers to do these activities with colleagues, even if only one or two. Nevertheless, an individual teacher determined to become aware of his or her mental processes can also benefit from these activities. In either case, it helps to have pen and paper at hand to capture reflections and make note of your reading processes.

Capturing Reading Processes

The key to this activity is to work with a text that is short (one or two pages) yet difficult enough to challenge all participants. To capture information about their own reading processes, teachers read the text to themselves, then share any problems they encountered and talk about the various problem-solving strategies they used to make sense of what they read.

As they talk they try to sort their reading processes into one of four general categories—fluency, motivation, cognition, and knowledge—as someone charts the comments on easel paper or an overhead transparency. The categories are defined as follows:

Fluency	Using automatic lower-level literacy: for example, decoding, word recognition, and sentence processing
Motivation	Setting purposes and goals; taking a stance as a reader; acknowledging affective responses to the text, task, or situation
Cognition	Monitoring attention; monitoring comprehension; using strategies (questioning, paraphrasing, summarizing, clarifying, rereading, imaging, and so forth) to focus attention and fix comprehension
Knowledge	World knowledge: drawing on and comparing to concepts, facts, or experience about topics
	Text knowledge: drawing on and comparing to knowledge of genre, text structures and features, language patterns, and conventions

The completed chart orients the teachers to the complexity of thinking actually involved in reading comprehension. Because it is often difficult to choose just one category for each comment, the teachers are reminded that the moves readers carry out in their heads while reading overlap and interact. This activity also highlights how a variety of proficient readers may approach the same difficult text in a variety of fashions, and it gives participants greater empathy for students, who approach assigned texts with many fewer resources than their teachers.

The following excerpt and Exhibit 9.1 show a text from the Academic Literacy course that we use in this activity with teachers and the chart that resulted.

Totalitarianism Turned Hate into Genocide

Throughout history, conquerors have burnt towns and killed their inhabitants or sent them into slavery. Prisoners have been tortured and confined in dungeons for religious or political reasons. Organizations such as the Inquisition developed interrogation and torture into a science. In particular Jewish people have suffered outbreak after outbreak of persecution and violence.

But while there have been many tyrants and persecutions in past centuries, mass murder was difficult. It took time to kill people one by one with sword or axe. Modern weapons such as the machine gun and poison gas vastly increased the destructive potential of war. Turned against a particular group of people within a country, these weapons could become the tools of genocide.

War and genocide require social organization on a large scale. As the 1900s began, tyrants not only acquired new weapons, they also seized hold of new tools for social organization and control. Radio could carry the leader's voice into every home and school. High-capacity printing presses could produce propaganda leaflets and posters. Thanks to the automobile, secret police could move swiftly and easily around the country. The telephone kept each headquarters in touch with the others, helping government officials to be organized enough to round up dissidents and smash opposition. The result is a totalitarian state in which nothing escapes the attention of the government.

Propaganda and Indoctrination Orchestrated Feelings

Perhaps the most important tools of the new totalitarian states were propaganda and indoctrination. By repeatedly playing on the peoples' hopes and fears, propaganda could whip people into a fever pitch of hatred for an external enemy—or for a group of people at home who were "different" or did not conform. People who supported the leader were portrayed as self-sacrificing heroes. The enemy or domestic opponents of the regime were pictured as devils or beasts who were corrupt and depraved. Once fully in power, totalitarian states quickly turned to *indoctrination,* or the systematic use of propaganda to form habits and attitudes. It is no coincidence that totalitarian states such as Nazi Germany, the Soviet Union, and Communist China took over complete control of children's education. Young people were often enrolled in special camps or movements such as the Hitler Youth. Children were even turned against their own parents, told to spy on them, and given rewards for turning them in to the authorities.

Fear and Isolation Paralyzed Resistance

As well-armed and powerful as they were, dictators could be overthrown if enough people rose up together. Alexander Solzhenitsyn, looking back at the Stalinist terror, in his book *The Gulag Archipelago*, reflected:

> And how we burned in the camps later, thinking: What would things have been like if every Security operative, when he went out at night to make an arrest, had been uncertain whether he would return alive and had to say good-bye to his family? Or if, during periods of mass arrests, as for example in Leningrad, when they arrested a quarter of the entire city, people had not simply sat there in their lairs, paling with terror at every bang of the downstairs door and at every step on the staircase, but had understood that they had nothing left to lose and had boldly set up in the downstairs hall an ambush of half a dozen people with axes, hammers, pokers, or whatever else was at hand? . . . Or what about the Black Maria [police wagon] sitting out there on the street with one lonely chauffeur—what if it had been driven off or its tires spiked? The [security] Organs would very quickly have suffered a shortage of officers and transport and, not withstanding all of Stalin's thirst, the cursed machine would have ground to a halt!

The problem is that a revolution is usually possible only after a prolonged period of unrest and gradually strengthening opposition. The dictators used terror to demoralize the people and made an example of any individual who protested. People stopped speaking out and organizing opposition when they saw protesters clubbed or gunned down in the streets, stores smashed, and newspapers closed. Dictators also took advantage of the fact that most people were slow to realize that the rule of law had ended, that guilt or innocence no longer mattered. As they were hauled off to the police headquarters, people thought, "It must be a mistake. I'm a good citizen. Surely everything will be straightened out."

Finally, even people who despised the new state were not united in their opposition to the dictator. As each group in turn bore the brunt of persecution, other groups comforted themselves because they were not Jews, or Communists, or other "enemies of the state!" By the time they heard the knock on their own doors, who was left to protest on their behalf?[1]

EXHIBIT 9.1

Four Interacting Areas of Reading: What Did You Do to Make Sense of This Text?

Fluency	Motivation	Cognition	Knowledge	
			World Knowledge	Text Knowledge
I had to stop and reread some of the really complex sentences.	When I saw Solzhenitsyn's name, I had a sinking feeling. I never could get through his books.	I found myself arguing with the text, because I thought Solzhenitsyn, even though it is used in the text, actually provided a counter-example to the overall position taken by the author of the text.	Of course I was thinking of Kosovo and what's happening now.	I looked at the caption under the picture before I read the text. It sort of clued me in to what would be there.
I stop cold at Solzhenitsyn's name because I know I can't pronounce (decode) it.	To tell you the truth, I wouldn't have read this if I wasn't in this situation, knowing I could draw on the social support of other readers.		I had movie images in mind.	I looked for the publication date because I wanted to see how recently this was written, what kind of slant it would probably take.
I had to break up a word into its parts to figure out what it really meant. I mean, take the root and suffix apart.	I only read this because I'm a "good student" and you asked me to.	I reread after I found I had blurred through a bunch of text without understanding it.	I remember some of Solzhenitsyn's speeches and when the *Gulag* was first published, the reviews of it.	I read all the titles and subtitles first.
		I realized I wasn't understanding what the author was getting at so I decided to read on until it cleared up.	Slavery came to mind. Tiananmen Square. Russia.	I was fascinated by some of the word choices the author made and spent some time thinking about the perspective of the text.
			When I came to the phrase "paralyzed resistance," I consciously decided to think about my own experience and other knowledge I might have that would make sense of that phrase.	

Think-Aloud Practice

Another of the reading activities we do with teachers is thinking aloud while reading a complex text. This is also aimed at helping make the ordinarily invisible process of reading more visible. We often start the thinking-aloud practice with an activity completely unrelated to reading, such as making animals out of Play-Doh or pipe cleaners. Working in pairs, teachers are asked to think out loud as they go about choosing which animal to make and then making it. The purpose of starting with something that is reasonably silly and that is not reading is twofold: to loosen participants up and start building camaraderie and to give participants the experience (which students often have when reading discipline-specific texts) of doing something unfamiliar, something they do not necessarily do with ease.

We then ask teachers to think aloud as they read. To again mirror the student experience, they read a text that requires some work for them to comprehend. Modern novels like *Sula*, by Toni Morrison, or *The God of Small Things*, by Arundhati Roy, are good selections because they demand a high level of reader engagement. Ideally, the text is also new to all the readers so that everyone is working to comprehend rather than simply recall it. Once again working in pairs, the teachers trade off, one reading excerpts from the text and thinking aloud about what he or she is doing to comprehend the text while the other listens. The following is a partial transcript of a reading activity in which one reader thinks aloud with *The Red Badge of Courage* by Stephan Crane.[2]

Thinking Aloud with *The Red Badge of Courage*

Reader: I have this image of, oh, the Civil War I guess, and, uh, I don't really have any preconceived notion of it, other than, uh, maybe some mixed-up image of *All's Quiet on the Western Front* or something, which is the next war. But I picture youth fighting, but this is Chapter One.

The cold passed reluctantly from the earth, and the retiring fogs revealed an army stretched out on the hills, resting.

Reader: Hmm, so they're already there, laid out on the ground waiting for the sun to rise, getting ready I guess for the next battle. Must be stepping in in the middle of it here.

As the landscape changed from brown to green, the army awakened, and began to tremble with eagerness at the noise of rumors.

Reader: So, sounds like they are waiting for instructions. They're about to move on and they're all, uh, anxious about that.

It cast its eyes upon the roads, which were growing from long troughs of liquid mud to proper thoroughfares.

Reader: "It" meaning the sun, I guess. It's warming up. I guess there are so many, there must be a lot of people, a lot of soldiers around, because they're tromping the mud into, uh, I can picture them tromping the dirt into mud and that into highways of soldiers.

A river, amber-tinted in the shadow of its banks, purled at the army's feet; and at night, when the stream had become of a sorrowful blackness, one could see across it the red, eyelike gleam of hostile camp-fires set in the low brows of distant hills.

Reader: So they're on the river bank, and I can picture them looking at the water and thinking two things. One, it's a river—it's pretty—and it's night, but, but, there are also these dark, there are these red eyes across, um, across the banks, that represent the enemy, which you know would just naturally make them more anxious.

Once a certain tall soldier developed virtues and went resolutely to wash a shirt. He came flying through a brook waving his garment bannerlike. He was swelled with a tale he had heard from a reliable friend, who had heard it from a truthful cavalryman,

Reader: A reliable friend, oop, I already said that,

who had heard it from the trustworthy brother, one of the orderlies at division headquarters.

Reader: Um, I thought he was going to be running from a bullet, but rather he's running from, running . . . *with* uh, hearsay, rumors of, per- haps where they're going and what they're going to be doing next.

He adopted the imported air, important air of a herald in red and gold.

Reader: So, he became sort of a standard-bearer with the news, and he's running among the soldiers.

"We're goin' t' move 't morrah—sure, he said pompously to a group in the com- pany street.

Reader: Sounds like with the dialogue we're trying to create a character who's either southern or at least countrified. Goes on to say:

We're goin' way up the river, cut across, an' come down in behint 'em."

Reader: Well, that's sort of country, but it's also sort of eighteenth- or nineteenth-century-speak, I guess.

To his attentive audience he drew a loud and elaborate plan of a very brilliant campaign. When he had finished, the blue-clothed men scattered into small argu- ing groups between the rows of squat brown huts.

Reader: He's uh, I don't know they talked about him speaking of a brilliant campaign, and he's basing this on hearsay, so he's obviously inflating his own importance in bearing this news.

A negro teamster who had been dancing upon a cracker box with the hilarious encouragement of twoscore soldiers was deserted.

Reader: So that, once again, paints a picture of nineteenth-century America with, uh, the white soldiers on one side and perhaps, just for comic relief, uh, one black man who's . . . who's, I have no idea what he does, what he's doing there except that he's been, he's, you know, forced to, no not forced, but he's just entertaining.

Close Reading

The close reading activity is similar to assignments such as reading logs and dialectical journals, which many teachers already use to actively engage their students with texts. But those activities focus on responses to content, whereas this one focuses on connecting the reading process to the content of the text. Specifically, teachers are asked to focus on how they know what they think they know about the content and, specifically, what in the text makes them think they know it. As they construct meaning from the text in front of them, participants consider what information and other clues are offered directly in the text and what knowledge about people, events, situations, or ideas is brought to the text by the reader. More important, readers are asked to identify what it is in the text—or about the text—that has prompted their inferences, assumptions, and associations.

Close reading helps teachers better understand how text interpretations emerge from the complex relationship between such things as the reader's strategies, the text's idiosyncratic features, the text's direct information, and the reader's prior knowledge.

We have used a variety of texts for the close reading activity, including "The Catbird Seat" by James Thurber and a *SLAM* magazine interview with Michael Jordan. After reading several paragraphs, readers answer two questions about each paragraph: What Do You Think You Know? and What in the Text Makes You Think You Know It? Here is a brief example.

Text for Close Reading

Mr. Martin bought the pack of Camels on Monday night in the most crowded cigar store on Broadway. It was theatre time and seven or eight men were buying cigarettes. The clerk didn't even glance at Mr. Martin, who put the pack in his overcoat pocket and went out. If any of the staff at F&S had seen him buy the cigarettes, they would have been aston-ished, for it was generally known that Mr. Martin did not smoke, and never had. No one saw him.[3]

What Do You Think You Know?	**What in the Text Makes You Think You Know It?**
OK, I think this is in New York	*Because it's crowded and it's Broadway.*
But I realize it could be, really be anywhere.	*But the theater time also makes me think that it's in New York.*
I think the store is F&S. But I'm not even sure about that.	*I think that's true because "if any of the staff at F&S had seen him" and "the clerk didn't even glance," so that's one person who didn't see him.*
	But I realize that F&S could be something else also. It could be the place where he worked and so . . . I don't know too much for sure there. Could be going to the theater, but no, not necessarily. So, I mostly have questions at this point.
I don't know that he smokes. So I don't know if he's starting to smoke or buying it for somebody else then. At this point in the paragraph, what I have are a lot of questions.	*I mean, it says he doesn't.*
I don't know if it's his writing here, but I think he's doing something perverse. He has a scheme. He's doing something that he normally does not do, and the author makes a point that he puts it in his overcoat pocket. Even though it didn't say he was concerned about not being seen, they pointed out	*Because of the overcoat.*

*that he was not seen. That implies
that he's doing something. . . .*

*It's interacting with the genre.
Because no one saw him could
be a very objective, trite statement.
But as you say, there's a lot of
implications that there is
something covert.*

*So there's that subtext.
Something out of the ordinary
that doesn't usually happen.
He's building a little bit of
a mystery.*

*So that "no one saw him" fits
in with that genre of "there's a
mystery here."*

*Whereas in another kind of a
genre, it wouldn't have that
implication.*

*You could even say that he wants
to be invisible.*

*He's in the most crowded place
on Broadway.*

Something surreptitious.

Uncovering Disciplinary Ways of Reading

We know that generally speaking, skilled readers set goals, use their background knowledge, question, picture, clarify, summarize, paraphrase, predict, monitor comprehension, and apply other strategies. But how do such reading strategies play out differently for readers in different disciplines? What idiosyncratic tools, knowledge, or expectations does a proficient reader of science texts bring to his or her reading that may differ from what a reader of history or literature brings? This activity aims at helping teachers develop a deeper understanding of what is involved in their own disciplinary reading, preparing them to better communicate the process to their students.

In this activity, teachers in the same subject area all tackle the same challenging discipline-specific text. A group of science teachers might read a difficult piece from *Science* or *Scientific American*. History teachers might read a recently published historical account or a college history textbook. Teachers of literature might choose a short story, drama, poem, or novel with which they are unfamiliar. An individual working alone can also embark on this type of inquiry in his or her own content area.

Once they have chosen a text, the teachers each record their answers to the following two questions: Before reading this text, what expectations do you have about it? and What predictions do you have about what you will be reading? This alone can be an interesting focus of inquiry. When experienced science readers began an article from *Scientific American,* they told us they knew it would review the current knowledge on its topic and end with a set of questions about the things that were still unknown. Some of them even skipped the introductory narrative, telling us they knew it would be irrelevant. When a literature teacher started to read this same article, however, she focused closely on the introductory narrative and did not expect the exposition that rapidly followed this opening.

Teachers then read the text to themselves for ten minutes as they would read any text of the same kind, feeling free to write in the margins and to underline or circle words. Afterward they record their responses to these questions in a journal:

1. What parts of this section of the text did you pay particular attention to? Why do you think you focused your attention on these parts?

2. What questions, if any, were you asking as you read?

3. What images, if any, were you forming as you read?

4. What predictions do you have about the remainder of the text, having read this much?

The group cycles at least once more through the process of reading the text and then writing responses to these four questions. Next the teachers review their notes individually, generalizing about their disciplinary reading in these areas:

1. The kinds of things they were paying particular attention to and the roles these things played in comprehending the text,

2. The kinds of questions they were asking themselves and the roles these questions played in comprehending the text,

3. The kinds of images they were forming and the roles these images played in comprehending the text, and

4. The kinds of predictions they were making and the knowledge or information on which they based the predictions.

After reviewing their reflections individually, the teachers share any patterns or generalizations they noticed about their own reading processes, with one participant recording generalizations on easel paper.

What emerges from this inquiry is the identification of some common ways that people in a discipline tend to approach certain texts of that discipline. When different subject area groups share their reading inquiries with one another, they are often surprised to see how ways of reading differ from one discipline to the next. All this sharing helps subject area teachers become more attuned to the tacit rules, ways of thinking, idiosyncratic vocabulary, and background knowledge needed to read effectively in their disciplines. This knowledge in turn prepares them to help their students learn to work more effectively with discipline-specific texts.

A Note on Process Versus Content

These four reading inquiry activities are designed to help teachers make their thinking public, to identify and bring to the surface the resources they bring to various kinds of texts. In our personal reading development, we have found it useful to conduct these inquiries multiple times with different kinds of texts. Doing so has helped us and others build a fuller vision of the different approaches to reading that a skilled reader has in his or her reading repertoire.

Of course this focus on reading is not meant to substitute for conversations about the substance and ideas in texts. It is an entirely different enterprise. However, we know that while exploring the reading process, adult readers often find it difficult to defer their responses to and connections with a text's world of ideas. We suggest two ways to cope with this need to address content directly. First, remind yourself and your fellow teachers of your purposes in conducting these inquiries: to experience and articulate how you, as proficient readers, make sense of texts. Second, allow time for a separate discussion about the ideas in the texts you have read together. Indeed, this discussion may yield further ideas about how to link process-focused and content-focused reading discussions in your classroom.

The Impact of Inquiry-Based Professional Development

We have found that teachers engaging collegially in the kinds of activities described here come to several realizations that can profoundly change the way they see themselves as readers, their teaching roles, and their students.

Seeing Reading Differently

As teachers practice articulating and describing their own reading processes, they discover that the act of reading is far more complex than it seems on the surface. They recognize that expert readers know how to skim to get an overview or gist of a piece, how to read in a focused way to answer a specific question, and how to organize the information they are reading into a mental map, or schema, that helps them retain what they are learning. They realize that expert readers can quickly judge the difficulty of a particular text and adjust their reading strategies accordingly. In other words, teachers who examine their own and others' reading come to appreciate it for the awe-inspiring accomplishment it really is. From that appreciation come some changes in how these teachers view their students and how they view their jobs. As one teacher wrote, "I now understand that reading is just as taxing as some of my students claim it to be. I understand that approaching a text can be intimidating even when you recognize all the words on the page. And I understand that reading involves more of the reader than I thought. As a result, much has changed in the way I think about texts and how to help my students interact with them."

Seeing and Hearing Students Differently

In our view, one of the most far-reaching results of reading apprenticeship is its power to change teacher-student relationships. Appreciating the complexity of the reading process often changes teachers' perspectives about their students. A deeper understanding of reading's inherent challenges, especially in discipline-specific texts, dispels the common assumption that students could be more successful readers "if only they tried harder." Teachers who in the past may have identified certain students as lazy or unmotivated come to recognize that these students may simply need more explicit help in mastering the complex set of mental activities required to comprehend academic and other difficult text. This understanding is an important early step in preparing teachers to support students' development as independent readers. As one teacher told us, "I now see that understanding does not come automatically, and I see all the steps that have to be gone through to engage students in a book." Another network teacher explained it this way: "Now I'm so aware of what students come with: reading conditions at home, background knowledge, past success or failure with reading. Now we talk about these things."

Teachers realize that students who struggle with reading may already be working very hard to make sense of what they encounter on the written page. They see that they can help these adolescents become more proficient readers by helping them acquire more powerful reading strategies and habits and a more extensive understanding of the codes and background knowledge essential for successful reading in particular disciplines. Most important, they see new ways of intervening in the problems they see students having in class. As one teacher said, "I am constantly aware of the reading process now, and what is happening to the kids. This has had a major impact on my interaction with the kids and the way I direct the literacy activities. It has changed the way I talk to a child who is having difficulties."

Seeing One's Job Differently

As noted before, many subject area teachers initially reject the notion that they can or should also be reading teachers. They see this not only as someone else's job but as irrelevant to helping students acquire subject area proficiency. But our experience tells us that when teachers start identifying the wealth of resources and knowledge they bring to their own discipline-specific reading, they begin thinking of themselves as *guides* into the content and the texts of their disciplines. They realize that if they can demystify the reading of subject area texts they will help students become more independent learners and gain a deeper understanding of the subject. And they come to see students' growing reading prowess as a powerful tool for learning their particular discipline. Gradually, the distinction between teaching reading and teaching the discipline begins to blur for these teachers; eventually, it disappears. One teacher told us, "I think I'm actually on a roll toward shifting my perception of myself as only a history/English teacher to that of a 'reading' teacher as well."

When subject area teachers take on the role of master reader in their respective disciplines, their classrooms feel different. We find that teachers who have assumed this role spend more time working explicitly with texts and allocate more classroom time to reading and talking about reading. They become models of and copractitioners in the processes they want students to learn rather than stage-front instructors. Active inquiry into reading tends to raise the classroom noise level, but it also raises comprehension. As students acquire the skills needed to become independent learners in a particular discipline, they ask more questions and have greater confidence in their own ability to construct meaning from texts.

Expanding the Reading Repertoire

Many teachers who participate in the Writing Project discover that coming to know oneself as a writer is interesting and rewarding on a personal level. Equally important, however, this new knowledge serves as a powerful resource in the work of helping students learn to write more like expert writers write. Similarly, teachers in the Strategic Literacy Network have found that taking an inquiry stance toward their own reading not only greatly benefits their work with students but also yields some rewarding, and unexpected, changes in their own reading habits.

As one teacher said, "I used to think of my reading as a competition of sorts—getting through as fast as possible. I've always been able to extrapolate meaning from small chunks of information, so I can fake comprehension from remembering bits of text. Now, though, I spend much more energy slowing down, rereading, and talking to myself and others about what I read. I like comprehending better than finishing." And as a veteran English teacher confided: "I enjoy reading what I call airplane books—books that would be page-turners if you had to be on an airplane for five hours. But since I've been in the network, I think my level of reading has gone up a notch or two. Now when I read books that I wouldn't have tolerated before because they weren't easy, I find myself saying, 'This is a terrific book, I can have an intelligent conversation with somebody about it.' I would say changes in my own reading have turned out to be one of the biggest bonuses of being in the network."

Note

1. L. S. Krieger and K. Neill, "Totalitarianism in the Modern World," in *Issues of the Modern Age* (D.C. Heath, 1994).

2. S. Crane, *The Red Badge of Courage: An Episode of the American Civil War* (London: William Heinemann, 1896).

3. J. Thurber, "The Catbird Seat," in *The Thurber Carnival* (New York: Harper & Row, 1931).

Chapter 10

Developing Schoolwide Reading Apprenticeship Programs

Never doubt that a small group of thoughtful, committed citizens can change the world. Indeed, it's the only thing that ever has.

Margaret Mead

SCHOOLWIDE EFFORTS to improve adolescents' reading can take many different forms. Examples include a stand-alone course along the lines of Academic Literacy, reading apprenticeship approaches embedded in classes across departments (such as English and Social Studies), reading across-the-curriculum, and reading in a "family" grouping of students. We have demonstrated that a stand-alone course like Academic Literacy (described in Chapters Three through Six) can result in profound, positive changes. We have shown that an embedded approach to reading apprenticeship in history, science, or English courses as described in Chapter Seven can also spark powerful progress in students' reading.

But in order to create a stand-alone course or to embed reading apprenticeship in more than one or two isolated classrooms, committed individuals must strategically advocate for and guide efforts toward creating a schoolwide program. In this final chapter we offer some suggestions for *making the case* (developing interest and support) and *building a base* (in teachers' professional community, in materials and curriculum development, in administrative support) for a schoolwide effort to improve students' reading based on the approach presented in this book.

Making the Case for Reading Apprenticeships

When a group of thoughtful, committed members of a school community has come to believe that there is a significant problem with students' reading, that this problem can be effectively addressed using elements of a reading apprenticeship approach, and that they can work with others to develop an organized response to the problem, they have begun to build a foundation for developing a schoolwide reading apprenticeship program.

In addition, this group of people must then persuade a critical mass of other members of their school community that

- Problems with students' reading are mostly problems of reading comprehension and engagement.

- Reading comprehension can be improved through explicit instruction and practice in reading comprehension strategies in the context of reading authentic texts.

- Reluctant adolescent readers can be (re-)engaged with reading through opportunities to read books of their own choosing, to become aware of their own reading preferences and processes, and to explore the role of reading in society and their futures.

- It is the job of subject area teachers to help students improve their ability to comprehend texts in their disciplines.

- Subject area teachers already know a great deal about reading in their disciplines and will be able—*if they begin to surface their invisible knowledge about reading*—to apprentice students as readers, helping them explore and expand their reading repertoire.

Analyzing the Problem

Gathering and examining data from a variety of sources to understand students' reading abilities and difficulties is a good first step toward developing a critical mass of people who share these understandings and are ready to take action. We suggest that advocates involve as many interested members of the school community as possible in an investigation of the question, *What is the state of our students' reading?* This investigation might include not only standardized test score data (disaggregated by ethnic groups, language proficiency, grades, gender, or any other ways relevant to your community) but also a variety of other data such as student reading surveys (see Appendix B: Reading Assessment), interviews or focus groups with students about their reading histories and habits, faculty surveys that include detailed information about typical reading assignments and expectations, and observations of students' reading capabilities and challenges.

Another way to gather information, as well as to create a broader constituency for addressing adolescents' reading development, is to involve the school's larger community. Advocates could develop surveys, focus groups, or other information-gathering methods to ask parents and employers in the community about their hopes, expectations, concerns, and observations related to young peoples' reading abilities and habits. Involving students themselves in gathering information from potential future employers about job-related reading requirements could be an important method of developing authentic student support for a reading improvement program.

School communities may find that, in addition to state- or district-mandated reading comprehension tests, other assessments like the Degrees of Reading Power (DRP) test, which reports students' reading comprehension keyed to lists of books at appropriate levels for students' reading, will yield information directly applicable to classroom planning and instruction. (For more information on the DRP, see Appendix B: Reading Assessment.) Finally, schools with access to reading specialists might plan to assess a cross section of students to have a more fine-grained understanding of their reading competencies and difficulties on which to base program development decisions.

Assessing Success

Positive results in student achievement will be the most persuasive evidence from which to argue that the trade-offs and efforts involved in implementing a reading apprenticeship approach across a middle school or high school are worthwhile. Advocates will need to develop and then implement a clear and workable evaluation plan. The driving question must be, How will we know if this effort is working? Or, to put it another way, What kind of success are we looking for, and what evidence will we use to measure that success?

The evaluation instruments we have used in assessing the impact of both the Academic Literacy course and the embedded reading apprenticeship approach of Strategic Literacy Network teachers have the benefit of being informative for classroom teachers as well as being quantifiable and meaningful to other audiences (see Appendix B: Reading Assessment).

Building the Base for Reading Apprenticeships Schoolwide

Whatever form a schoolwide program takes, the most important aspect of building a base is to develop support for teachers in incorporating reading apprenticeship into their classrooms. To achieve substantial and lasting classroom changes, ideas and practices that can transform teaching and learning need to take root in the hearts and minds of individual teachers.

Middle and high school teachers see their primary responsibility as conveying the content of their subject area. The idea of teaching reading as an integral aspect of teaching the content of their subject area may require persuasion—persuasion that this approach can make a difference for their students and will not require them to add new curriculum.

We strongly recommend that teachers be presented with opportunities to learn about but *not* mandated to implement a reading apprenticeship approach in their classrooms. Most emphatically, teachers should not be assigned to teach a stand-alone course unless they are committed to these ideas. When an apprenticeship model is the central metaphor for teaching and learning, teachers must be able to engage students in questions such as *How do we make sense of this passage?* in a genuine spirit of inquiry. Mandating teachers to take this kind of approach undermines the likelihood of developing classrooms in which apprenticeship and inquiry can flourish.

Building a Professional Community of Teachers

The key to creating teachers' learning communities that can positively affect student learning is to develop ongoing professional conversation focused on problem solving—exploring specific teaching and learning issues. In teachers' learning communities that we develop and nurture, we create opportunities and support for a particular kind of professional learning. In professional conversations, teachers engage in building a theoretically and experientially grounded knowledge base that serves as a deep, internalized reference point. This kind of professional learning has played a key role in changing individual teachers' attitudes, beliefs, and classroom practices in ways that have produced significant, positive student learning outcomes.[1]

In these professional conversations a common language and set of understandings evolves and is tested and refined through cycles of classroom practice and feedback.

We have found professional development to be most productive when meetings include, with regard to content, (1) a common basis for the conversation through shared students, projects, goals, curriculum, or a shared analysis of student work and (2) a variety of data and perspectives on classroom teaching and learning, including student work, videotapes of teaching, current research, and teachers' own personal and professional experiences. With regard to process, the following should be included: (1) routines for reflection and exchange of ideas, resources, and problem solving; (2) inquiry processes for exploring classroom issues and data; and (3) a clear set of agreed-upon ground rules for the discussion and individuals prepared to facilitate conversation with these ground rules in mind.

Making the Time for Professional Community

Whether a school is trying to institute a course similar to Academic Literacy or to incorporate reading apprenticeships across the curriculum or to do both, time is of paramount importance. Participating teachers will need more than an interest in improving students' reading. They will need time for the relevant professional development, continuing learning opportunities with disciplinary experts, curriculum planning, and collaborative refinement of both curriculum and practice that will make the program successful. Overall, few schools and districts in the United States have been able to give teachers adequate time for such things. Yet, this is the kind and level of teacher support that could actually help today's students achieve the "world-class standards" that increasing numbers of state boards of education and legislatures are adopting. For most educators, the idea that schools are places where teachers as well as students are expected to and supported to engage in ongoing learning has yet to become a reality.

Despite fiscal concerns and some thorny issues related to child care for working parents who are stranded by student-free school days, there is a growing consensus that building regular and significant professional development time into teachers' work schedules is crucial.[2] An increasing number of schools and districts are developing innovative ways to create more time for teachers to work and learn together professionally.[3] In middle and high schools, these include *block scheduling, banking time,* and state or district staff development days during which students are not in school. Some districts are developing contractual agreements in which teachers are paid for more days per calendar year, with professional development time either front-loaded (where teachers meet for several days or weeks before classes begin), back-loaded (where teachers meet for several days or weeks after the school year ends), or otherwise integrated throughout a longer teaching year.

In schools where the faculty is able to meet for significant periods of professional development time across the curriculum, teachers or leadership teams (including teachers) can organize reading process sessions based on the ideas and processes described in Chapter Nine. Schools interested in developing a schoolwide focus on improving reading across the curriculum can also use department meetings as opportunities for this kind of professional learning related to discipline-specific reading. In fact, when there is not yet a schoolwide commitment, a single department might decide to begin by integrating reading instruction into its classes. Here, too, department meetings are the logical place for the necessary professional development and planning.

Developing Materials and Curriculum Plans

Well-stocked classroom and school libraries are critical to building the engagement and fluency of adolescent readers. Although school libraries receive basic funding from the school budget, building a classroom library can take more creativity and effort. At the classroom level, teachers can initiate book drives in which parents, students, and even other faculty solicit used books from their neighborhoods and local businesses. At the school level, a book fair, usually sponsored by a local book store, can provide students and parents with the opportunity to buy books, either for home or for the student's classroom, with any profits going to buy more books for the school library. It is vitally important that these classroom libraries contain books representing a wide variety of genres, including nonfiction of various kinds, a good representation of books that include characters and topics related to students' cultural experiences, a variety of topics of interest to youth, and a sizable range of difficulty levels.

After the question of materials, the next pressing question for teachers, especially teachers creating a stand-alone course, will be the question of curriculum scope and sequence. In planning this type of course, designers should address the four key dimensions of a reading apprenticeship classroom (social, personal, cognitive, and knowledge resources) and engage students in a set of consistent classroom routines that help establish and build their skills and engagement in reading a variety of texts. Most important, the course design should develop and build a metacognitive conversation about reading that will provide a consistent vehicle for reading instruction in the context of making sense of course texts.

In Chapter Three as well as Appendix A: Academic Literacy Curriculum, we present overviews of the way the Academic Literacy course integrated key ideas about reading and key strategies with the three units taught in the 1996–97 school year. Other school teams in the Strategic Literacy Network are using different texts and different thematic units and have developed their own, distinct ways of integrating the key ideas and key strategies.

When embedding reading apprenticeships into existing subject area courses, we recommend that educators begin by outlining the content of the curriculum. If we view curriculum development as weaving cloth, the curriculum content is the *warp*. Using the existing curriculum units and texts as a starting point, consider where and how to weave the *woof* of the fabric—the key dimensions and routines of reading apprenticeship (see Chapter Two)—into the content curriculum.

As Chapter Four and parts of Chapter Seven describe, the starting point for developing a reading apprenticeship classroom is to lay the groundwork for a learning environment that supports risk taking, collaboration, joint inquiry, and self-awareness in the beginning of the course.

Once teachers have integrated ways of engaging students in metacognitive conversations and have created ongoing classroom routines to reinforce these metacognitive practices early in the course, they can then introduce specific cognitive strategies (see Chapters Five and Seven) and knowledge-building strategies (see Chapters Six and Seven) into the curriculum.

Gaining Administrative Support

Teachers clearly have first-line responsibility in the reading apprenticeship approach. But administrative support is essential for the success of any schoolwide implementation of reading apprenticeship.

Managing and defending resources—again starting with time—is perhaps the most important role administrators can take. Teachers need time to develop their knowledge and skill as master readers and to come to understand how other experienced readers approach various texts differently. School scheduling is a sensitive business; administrators must be able to argue the benefits of professional development and planning time to a variety of audiences—parents, school board members, local news reporters, and perhaps even to the local media. In addition to time, administrators need to find and allocate monetary resources for development of materials and in some cases for outside assistance with professional development.

Along with allocating the necessary time and money, administrators must be advocates for reading apprenticeship. They may need to talk with students who are unhappy about having to take a course that is "just about reading" or with parents who are concerned that "my child's teacher is moving too slowly through the history textbook; I'm worried he won't learn everything he needs to do well on the state test."

Part of this advocacy should include discussion with members of the school community about the trade-offs involved in using a reading apprenticeship approach, the costs compared to the envisioned benefits. This is perhaps especially important in creating a new course, particularly one that will be required. Administrators must be prepared to make a persuasive case for its importance, describing the rationale behind the approach and anticipated benefits.

Last but certainly not least, administrative support might well require defending teachers using a reading apprenticeship approach from criticism from school board, district, or state officials who believe that a phonics-based approach is a better choice for secondary readers. As the debate about the best methods of teaching beginning reading moves beyond the early grades, the phonics versus whole language debate is also beginning to replicate. Administrators should be able to articulate the research and understand the rationale underlying the reading apprenticeship approach (see Chapters One and Two) so they can effectively persuade and support members of the school community whose cooperation will be crucial for success.

Conclusion: Crisis and Opportunity

The *quiet crisis* of adolescent literacy has grown louder in the year it has taken us to write this book. The front page of the August/September 1999 issue of *Reading Today*, the International Reading Association's bimonthly newspaper, announced: "Adolescent Literacy Comes of Age." The article cites the pervasive neglect of adolescent reading and the lack of resources and specialists at the secondary level, and describes a crisis in adolescent literacy "the magnitude of which is yet to be fully measured."[4] In presenting a new IRA resolution on adolescent literacy, the article argues that adolescent reading is an educational issue whose time has come. "At the start of the millennium, few people needed literacy skills. As a new one approaches, everyone does—young children, mature adults, and perhaps most importantly the adolescents who are beginning to find themselves and explore their place in the world."

This IRA resolution[5] calls for preparing teachers to respond to the escalating literacy needs of adolescent readers. Specifically, the resolution argues for the rights of adolescent readers, among them the right to have

- Instruction that builds both the skill and the desire to read increasingly complex material

- Qualified teachers who model and provide explicit instruction in reading comprehension, critical reading, and studying strategies across the curriculum and who understand the complexities of individual adolescents, respect their differences, and respond to their unique characteristics

- Homes, communities, and a nation that will not only support the efforts to achieve advanced levels of literacy but also provide the resources necessary for them to succeed.

In this book we have offered an instructional framework for reading apprenticeship that was developed and refined through a teacher-researcher collaborative effort. As a result of this work, classrooms of diverse middle school and high school students who were behind their age mates nationally not only developed as readers during the school year but actually exceeded normal rates of growth. They grew into more discriminating and strategic readers, empowered to choose their own recreational reading with increased knowledge about themselves as readers and with reference to a world of books and a community of other readers. Moreover, many of these students developed the knowledge and confidence to use a variety of cognitive tools to plough their way through difficult texts that would previously have seemed inaccessible to them.

There is cause for optimism here. Evidence that a range of middle and high school subject area teachers can foster significant schoolwide improvement in students' reading creates an opportunity for others to adapt and go beyond the successes described here. But optimism and opportunity must be accompanied by expanded effort. The vision we hold—that these students and students like them can break through the literacy ceiling limiting their current and future options—can become a reality only if they are served throughout their school years by teachers with enough knowledge, commitment, and confidence about teaching reading to facilitate their development as strategic readers. We have seen that teachers and their adolescent students bring many untapped resources to the classroom that can be tapped to empower students as more independent, critical, and engaged readers.

Making this vision a reality will require other productive teacher-researcher collaborations to mutually enrich theory and practice in adolescent reading. As we close this book, we want to once again encourage our readers to join us in this timely and rewarding work.

Notes

Epigraph: Quote attributed to American anthropologist Margaret Mead in *The Whole World Book of Quotations* (Addison Wesley, 1994), p. 33.

1. C. Greenleaf, R. Schoenbach, L. Morehouse, M. Katz, and F. Mueller. "Close Readings: Developing Inquiry Tools and Practices for Generative Professional Development." Paper presented at the annual meeting of the American Educational Research Association, Montreal, Apr. 1999.

2. See, for example, S. J. Rosenholtz, *Teachers' Workplace: The Social Organization of Schools* (New York: Teachers College Press, 1991); M. Fullan, "Change Processes in Secondary Schools, Towards a More Fundamental Agenda," in M. McLaughlin, J. Talbert, and N. Bascia (eds.), *The Contexts of Teaching in Secondary Schools: Teachers' Realities* (New York: Teachers College Press, 1990); M. McLaughlin and J. Talbert, *Contexts That Matter for Teaching and Learning:*

Strategic Opportunities for Meeting the Nation's Educational Goals (Stanford, Calif.: Center for Research on the Context of Secondary School Teaching, Stanford University, 1993); M. McLaughlin and D. Marsh, "Staff Development and School Change," in A. Lieberman (ed.), *Schools as Collaborative Cultures: Creating the Future Now* (London: Falmer Press, 1990); J. W. Little, "Teachers' Professional Development in a Climate of Educational Reform," *Educational Evaluation and Policy Analysis,* 1993, *15* (2), 129–151; D. Schön, "Professional Knowledge and Reflective Practice," in T. Sergiovanni and J. Moore (eds.), *Schooling for Tomorrow* (Boston: Allyn & Bacon).

3. National Education Commission on Time and Learning, *Prisoners of Time* (Washington, D.C.: U.S. Government Printing Office, 1994); J. Z. Aronson, *Ending the Tyranny of Time in Education* (San Francisco, Far West Laboratory, 1995).

4. *Reading Today,* Aug./Sept. 1999, Vol. 17, No. 1.

5. IRA Resolution on Adolescent Literacy, May 1999, International Reading Association Web site.

Epilogue

Inviting Continuing Conversation

WE HAVE SHARED with you an approach to reading development that has the potential to reengage secondary students as readers, to develop both their strategic reading repertoire and their control of reading comprehension, and to give them access to academic texts across the disciplines. We have described our implementation of this approach and also how we involve teachers and students in an inquiry into reading.

We are clearly enthusiastic about the rich potential of reading apprenticeships. But we are also well aware that there is no magic bullet for addressing the full set of complex issues that affect how well and how eagerly students read. Those issues range from student motivation, which is often influenced by students' perceptions about education and economic opportunity, to the grinding pressures teachers feel to prepare students to succeed on demanding high-stakes exams on the one hand and to work with students' real needs and diverse abilities on the other. Reading apprenticeships do not directly address such issues. But collegial inquiry into reading can lead to broader exchanges about how to approach the many difficult issues that ultimately affect secondary reading.

The reading apprenticeship approach was developed in an ongoing professional learning community of teachers and researchers based at WestEd, in San Francisco. As this book goes to press, we are expanding the reach of our professional community by developing a cadre of teacher-leaders who are able to share this work with others throughout the country by means of professional development series, conference presentations, publications, and electronic communication.

As our professional community grows, we are tapping into new and inventive ideas from the many talented and resourceful educators in our nation's schools. As a result, our knowledge and understanding of how to assist secondary students in becoming more powerful and engaged academic readers is growing.

We would like to hear more about what you are doing. We would like to collect from teachers and share with teachers

- More examples of ways to build fluency for adolescents without stigmatizing them as poor readers.

- More models for providing the extra support some students need.

- More examples of ways reading can serve the needs of second language learners and more about the materials that should be part of the classroom library for these students.

- More ways of working with young people to help them develop identities as readers.

- More ways to locate the resources teachers need, in this time of tight budgets and public skepticism, to help all students access a variety of texts.

- More ways to set time aside in subject area classes for reading ancillary materials.

- More ways for teachers, departments, districts, and school communities to make decisions in tandem about the kinds of compromises they are willing to accept to make room for reading in the subject area curriculum.

- More experiences that teachers have had with testing in different disciplines, districts, and states.

- More connections or disparities that teachers have seen between students' comprehension of discipline-based texts and their learning of a discipline.

Our Web site is [www.wested.org/stratlit]. It offers classroom ideas from Strategic Literacy Network teachers, some of the research documents referenced in this book, and links to other Web sites of interest to those working to support adolescent literacy development. We invite you to join our professional community. Please visit and share with us any knowledge, ideas, or experiences that you think might help all educators be better prepared to help secondary students gain control of academic texts and, in the process, become lifelong readers.

Appendix A
Academic Literacy Curriculum

This appendix contains a curriculum overview of the first unit, Reading Self and Society, taught in the Academic Literacy course. It then presents a one-page overview (Exhibit A.1) of the way in which components of the course were introduced and sustained throughout the three units taught in the 1996–1997 academic year.

Unit One: Reading Self and Society
Unit Description
This twelve-week unit engages students in inquiry into the personal and public worlds of reading through guided reflection into their own reading histories and experiences as well as those of others. The unit focuses on acquiring tools of more powerful literacy and on the relation of literacy to personal power, educational goals, and working lives. Texts are seen as "devised" or "constructed" in particular times and places for specific purposes and agendas, as selectively including and excluding particular readers, and as fallible sources of information.

Essential Questions
What is reading? What do proficient readers do when they read? What are my characteristics as a reader? What strategies do I use as I read? What role does reading serve in people's personal and public lives? What role will reading play in my future educational and career goals? What goals can I set and work toward to help myself develop as a reader?

Texts/Materials

Marilyn Jager Adams, "What Skillful Readers Know" in *Beginning to Read: Thinking and Learning about Print*

Rudolfo A. Anaya, "Seis" in *Bless Me, Ultima*

"What Is Reading?" in *Becoming a Nation of Readers*

James Baldwin, "If Black English Isn't a Language, Then Tell Me, What Is? in *Diverse Identities, Classic Multicultural Essays*

Claude Brown, "I Heard a Knock on the Door" from *Manchild in the Promised Land*

Emily Dickinson, "He Ate and Drank the Precious Words" and "There Is No Frigate Like a Book"

"Learning to Read and Write" in *Narrative of the Life of Frederick Douglass, an American Slave*

June Jordan, "Nobody Mean More to Me Than You and the Future of Willie Jordan" in *Diverse Identities, Classic Multicultural Essays*

Alfred Kazin, "The Word Was My Agony" from *A Walker in the City*

Maxine Hong Kingston, "Silence" in *Diverse Identities, Classic Multicultural Essays*

Bernard Malamud, "A Summer's Reading" from *The Magic Barrel*

Nicholasa Mohr, "The English Lesson" in *Hear My Voice: A Multicultural Anthology of Literature from the United States*

Richard Rodriguez, "On Becoming a Chicano" in *Patterns Across the Disciplines*

Mike Rose, "I Just Wanna Be Average" and "Entering the Conversation" in *Lives on the Boundary*

Kevin Clarke interview in *Speaking of Reading*

Richard Wright, "I Hungered for Books" from *Black Boy*

Malcolm X, "Learning to Read" in *Autobiography of Malcolm X*

Strategies/Skills Introduced
Cognitive Strategies

Staged introduction and guided practice with reciprocal teaching beginning with a focus on questioning and summarizing and followed by a focus on clarifying and predicting. The reciprocal teaching is scaffolded through varying degrees of teacher dependence to independent performance—teacher modeling, whole-class discussion, partnered reading, small-group discussions, individual testing of mastery.

- Questioning
- Summarizing
- Predicting
- Clarifying

Reading to Learn

Introduction to text-readiness and text-wiseness, through self-inquiry and guided use of specific skills for activating and elaborating background knowledge of a topic or field.

- Survey of reading history, habits, and attitudes
- Description of study environment and log
- Keeping a learning log
- Give One, Get One
- Annotating a text

Writing to Learn

Use of specific writing strategies to explore and extend one's thinking.

- Reflection on the ideas in a text, on relationships between these ideas and one's own experience, and on one's own processes of reading, through free writes and double-entry journals
- Note-taking strategies

Language Skills and Strategies

Introduction to academic terminology through the "language of inquiry" and specific terms for reading processes. Introduction to distinctions between dialects and edited or academic English (Standard English, the language of business and commerce, and so on).

- Question words and families (fact, interpretation, opinion, judgment, inference, question, inquiry, and so forth)
- Reading words and families (literacy, comprehension, decoding, process, language, dialect, vocabulary, and so forth)
- Distinction between dialect and standard, appropriate usage

Research Skills

Introduction to inquiry processes and sources of information.

- Generating questions to guide inquiry
- Getting information from self, texts, and others

- Summarizing information
- Evaluating information
- Interviewing techniques

Assignments, Products, and Performances

Choose an appropriate book for silent sustained reading (SSR)
Maintain a reflective reading log for SSR
Create a profile of self as a reader

- Survey of reading history, habits, and attitudes
- Description of study environment
- Study environment log
- Learning journal assignments

Draft and revise a reflective description of self as reader

- Written metaphor for reading
- SSR reading goals
- Study environment goals
- Analysis of strengths and weaknesses as a reader
- Mastery of reading strategy goals

Keep a unit learning log
Participate in reciprocal teaching reading discussions
Maintain word family study sheets
Complete writing to learn assignments

- Reflecting (free writes, double-entry response) on content of a text as well as on reading process
- Annotating
- Note taking

Individual interview of a reader
Assemble and reflect on reading portfolio

Writing in Various Genres

Definition (of a good book, of a good reader)
Metaphor (for reading)
Description of a place (study environment), of a process (reading)
Description (of self as a reader)
Summary

Evaluation
Personal reflection essay
Opinion essay

Reading and Writing Assessment

Reading portfolios as records of growth, including

- Profile of self as reader
- Individual reading plan and goals
- Ongoing metacognitive reflections on reading processes
- Selections from unit learning logs
- SSR log
- SSR project
- Records on movement toward reading goals
- Reflection, self-assessment, and evaluation of progress
- Cloze passages
- Demonstration of mastery of reciprocal teaching roles
- Reciprocal teaching test of individual performance
- Written reflections, unit logs, journals
- Annotations
- Reflective essay on self as reader
- Written summaries
- Interview questions
- Interviews and interview summaries
- Reading survey

EXHIBIT A.1

A Yearlong Course in Academic Literacy: Embedded Components

Sep	Oct	Nov	Dec	Jan	Feb	Mar	Apr	May	Jun

Unit 1: Reading Self and Society (Sep)
Unit 2: Reading Media (Dec)
Unit 3: Reading History (Mar)

Inquiry into self as reader, assessment and evaluation of reading strategies, sharing with classroom community through talk and written reflections

- Finding and assessing books using the "ten-page chance"
- Silent Sustained Reading (SSR) of a 200-page book per month
- SSR Logs with metacognitive writing about reading process
- Activating background knowledge, building schema
- Questioning strategies (QAR, ReQuest)
- Approaching unknown words (using context cues, assessing familiarity, analyzing word parts)
- Summarizing
- Predicting using text signals
- Clarifying (rereading, reading on)
- Reciprocal teaching (RT) procedure
- Chunking (parsing) complex sentences
- Analyzing rhetorical appeals, symbolism, construction of media and texts
- Previewing and prereading a text
- Paraphrasing
- Using graphic organizers, tree diagrams
- Locating main ideas in exposition
- Interpreting primary sources

Appendix B
Reading Assessment

The evaluation instruments we have used have the benefit of being informative for classroom teachers as well as quantifiable and meaningful to broader audiences. They are the Degrees of Reading Power test and the Pre-Course and Post-Course Reading Surveys.

Quantitative Measure of Reading Improvement: The Degrees of Reading Power Test

To evaluate the impact of the Academic Literacy course on student reading development and, later, the impact of the reading apprenticeship approach embedded in subject area classes, we wanted to measure changes in student reading processes. We also wanted the assessment to demand little from the teachers in the way of time, yet yield information useful in instructional decision making. Because we were not planning to conduct a controlled study, we sought a norm-referenced test that would measure ninth-grade student performance and progress against that of a larger population of similar students. The Degrees of Reading Power (DRP) test, from Touchstone Applied Science Associates, came closest to meeting these various criteria.

The DRP test is already used by several states and districts across the United States. It employs a modification of the *cloze* reading activity (described in Chapter Six), asking students to supply missing words in nonfiction paragraphs by choosing from a provided list of words. The omitted words are all common words, even though the passage may be difficult; thus failure to respond correctly should indicate failure to comprehend the passage rather than failure to understand the response options. In this way, unlike most standardized reading tests that ask students to show how much they comprehend by answering multiple-choice questions after they finish reading, the DRP focuses on how well students can construct meaning as they read. It measures students' ability to "process and understand increasingly more difficult prose material," focusing on student comprehension of the surface meaning of texts in order to measure "the process of reading rather than products of reading such as main idea and author purpose."[1]

Student performance on DRP tests is reported on a readability scale (of DRP units), which describes the most difficult text the student is expected to read with different levels of comprehension.[2] Perhaps the most notable omission in these scales, or indices, is that they do not treat the reader's interest or background knowledge relevant to the topic as a factor in understanding. Nevertheless they do give a standard against which student reading ability can be measured and give the teacher some idea of the kinds of texts students may be able to read with various degrees of comprehension. Also student scores can be easily converted to national percentiles and Normal Curve Equivalent scales for statistical comparisons.

The DRP helped us answer the question, Do students who have been in a course designed to engage them in problem solving to comprehend text perform better at a well-known comprehension task as a result of the course?

Qualitative Measures of Reading Improvement: Pre-Course and Post-Course Surveys

Before and after the 1996–97 Academic Literacy course we administered a survey to students, asking them to respond in their own words about their beliefs, reading habits, and attitudes. At the end of the year, students (and their teachers) were able to reflect on changes the students had made by looking at both surveys. A number of useful surveys exist, and teachers and schools often make up their own surveys to meet their unique informational needs. We used a survey adapted from Nanci Atwell, available as Appendix E in her book, *In the Middle*.[3] Again, we were interested not only in tracking changes that occurred but also in providing teachers with information useful for planning activities and for making recommendations to individual students.

1. If you had to guess, how many books would you say you owned?

2. How many books would you say are in your house?

3. How many novels would you say you've read in the last twelve months?

4. How did you learn to read?

5. Why do people read?

6. What does someone have to do in order to be a good reader?

7. Do you consider yourself a good reader? Why or why not?

8. What kinds of books do you like to read?

9. How do you decide which books you'll read?

10. Have you ever reread a book? If so, can you name it/them here?

11. Do you ever read novels at home for pleasure? If so, how often do you read at home for pleasure?

12. Who are your favorite authors?

13. Do you like to have your teacher read to you? If so, is there anything special you'd like to hear?

14. In general, how do you feel about reading?

Assessment of the Academic Literacy Course, 1996–97

DRP Results

Academic Literacy students were tested with one form of the DRP test at the end of October and seven months later, at the end of May, with a parallel form of the test.[4]

- As a group, these ninth graders gained 4 points (DRP units), a significantly greater amount than one year's expected growth at the ninth-grade level $t = 7.558$, df = 215, $p = .000$).

- The gain corresponded to an increase in students' independent reading level from the ability to read a text like *Charlotte's Web* (50 DRP units) to the ability to read a text like *To Kill a Mockingbird* (54 DRP units).

- When special education students' scores were removed from the group, the independent reading level began with the ability to read a text like *Old Yeller* (51 DRP units) and increased to the ability to read a text like *The Adventures of Tom Sawyer* (55 DRP units).

- In terms of ability to do independent reading of trade materials, students moved from the ability to read children's magazines to the ability to read teen fiction and adult fiction magazines.

- Students' instructional reading level reached a mean of 66 DRP units in the spring of 1997, corresponding to the ability to read texts like *The Prince* (65 DRP units) and *The Scarlet Letter* (67 DRP units).

- With instructional support, these students should be able to manage all but the most difficult of high school textbooks (50 percent of high school textbooks are rated at 62 to 68 DRP units).

- Percentile scores increased over 2 points from fall to spring, from 48.11 percent (below the national norm) to 50.41 percent (above the national norm) t = 2.152, df = 202, p = .031).

All groups of students made impressive gains from fall to spring, without regard to ethnicity or language background (see Chapter Three). There were no significant differences across the various teachers' classes, indicating that differences among teachers did not result in differences in student learning.

Survey Results

Students' responses on the Pre-Course and Post-Course Surveys showed distinct increases in the behaviors and attitudes we wanted students to acquire in order to begin to see themselves as proficient readers. Here is a sampling of their answers.

How many novels would you say you've read in the last twelve months? On the Pre-Course Survey students reported reading an average of 5.58 novels in the previous year; on the Post-Course Survey they reported reading an average of 10.99 books during the current year.

What does someone have to do in order to be a good reader? On the Pre-Course Survey, 71 percent of the students said one had to practice reading; on the Post-Course Survey they referred to many more ways to improve:

Twice as many said that a person must understand what he or she reads.

Over twice as many mentioned specific strategies good readers must use to make sense of what they read.

Twice as many thought that to become good readers people must enjoy reading and pick books that interest them.

How do you decide which books you'll read? The number of students who described previewing a book in order to decide whether to read it nearly doubled from the Pre-Course to the Post-Course Survey. By spring, 80 percent (134 students) had sampled a book by either skimming its pages or reading parts of it to see if they liked it.

Who are your favorite authors? Forty-two percent of the students could not name one favorite author in the Pre-Course Survey, but in the Post-Course Survey only 20 percent could not name a favorite author.

In general, how do you feel about reading? In the Pre-Course Survey, 42 percent of the students said they liked or loved reading, 38 percent said it was OK, and 17 percent said they did not enjoy it. In the Post-Course Survey, 67 percent of the students said they liked or loved reading, 27 percent said it was OK, and only 6 percent said they did not enjoy it.

A comparison of students' answers revealed that students had begun to think about reading less as a set of skills that they either had or did not have and more as a sense-making activity that they could control by using reading strategies and choosing books they liked. Their responses demonstrated that over the course of the school year they acquired a much more elaborate set of reading ideas, strategies, and resources and a greater sense of their own agency, responsibility, and control in relation to how they read. They grew more knowledgeable about selecting books to read, knew how to create reading situations that worked for them, and valued reading in new ways.

Assessment of Learning Outcomes in SLN Subject Area Classrooms

During the 1997–98 school year, the Strategic Literacy Initiative at WestEd convened the Strategic Literary network (SLN)—interdisciplinary teams of middle and high school teachers—for a series of professional development sessions based on a reading apprenticeship approach.

As a group, SLN middle school students significantly increased in average raw score from 42.2351 in the Fall to 45.7252 in the Spring ($t = -9.931$, df $= p < .000$), an average gain of 3.5 points. This corresponds to an average independent reading level of 47 DRP units in the Fall, increasing to 50 DRP units in the Spring. Against a norming population of age-matched peers, these students made a significant nearly 3-point gain in normal curve equivalence scores (FNCE $= 46.7980$, SNCE $= 49.5232$, $t = 5.462$, df $= 293$, $p < .000$). In terms of their national ranking, the middle school students began the year at the 43.81th percentile and moved to the 47.38th percentile by Spring ($t = 5.163$, df $= 293$, $p < .000$). Overall, these increases show SLN teachers closing the achievement gap between diverse, urban middle school students and the norming population of grade-matched peers.[*]

---

[*]DRP scores are reported as raw scores, then interpolated into a national percentile ranking as well as a normal curve equivalent score. Of these, only the normal curve equivalent scores meet the strictest criteria for statistical analysis using t tests, namely, distribution along equal intervals on a normal curve. For this reason, statistical analysis of NCE scores is most robust, and we can be most confident of results using this measure. However, the raw scores and percentile rankings are distributed along a nearly normal curve, making t tests of statistical significance accurate enough for the purpose of determining whether the gains in student reading scores are attributable to chance. Raw scores are also interpolated onto a readability scale, the DRP unit scale, which is criterion referenced, matched to text of particular difficulty levels.

SLN high school students, as a group, significantly increased in average raw score from 45.7639 in the Fall to 49.3750 in the Spring ($t = -4.487$, df = 71, $p < .000$), an average gain of 3.61 points. This corresponds to an average independent reading level of 54 DRP units in the Fall, increasing to 57 DRP units in the Spring. Against a norming population of age-matched peers, these high school students started close to the norm, yet made a significant nearly 2-point gain in normal curve equivalence scores (FNCE = 49.5556, SNCE = 51.5417, $t = -2.111$, df = 71, $p < .038$). In terms of their national ranking, the high school students began the year at the 48.76th percentile and moved above the 50th percentile to the 51.78th percentile by the Spring ($t = -2.201$, df = 70, $p < .031$). Overall, these increases show that even with a higher-achieving population of high school students, SLN teachers help these urban, diverse students to develop as readers, outstripping the norming population of grade-matched peers.

In general the students who had the most need of reading development (lower-scoring students, ESL students, and special education students) made the most gains. Students in English/Language Arts classes made more gains than those in history classes. When teachers using a reading apprenticeship approach had students for two periods a day, as they did at the middle school (in the English and Reading CORE classes), students made greater gains as well. Other factors, such as the exact strategies the teachers were implementing and the frequency of strategy implementation, are clearly important to explore as we continue to work to understand where and what the key leverage points may be for accelerating student reading ability in the context of subject area instruction.

Although these data represent small numbers of children for each participating teacher, they show a strong and suggestive trend. We believe these outcomes are remarkable for several reasons. First, they occur among a population of urban students who are among the nation's most impoverished youth. They occur despite the prior history of school failure of many of these children. They occur among a population of children whose first language is typically not English. And critically, they occur not among the students of a special class focused on reading but among the students of subject area classes of teachers struggling with new teaching approaches, trying to implement research-proven ways to support reading development as they also teach a literature or history curriculum mandated by their district and state.

Notes

1. Touchstone Applied Science Associates, *DRP Handbook: G&H Test Forms* (Brewster, N.Y.: Touchstone Applied Science Associates, 1995), pp. 1, 11.

2. The DRP readability scale indexes the relative proportion of common or frequently used words in the text, the relative proportion of short to long words in the text, and the relative length and complexity of sentences in the text. A mathematical formula based on the Bormuth mean cloze readability formula (Touchstone Applied Science Associates, *DRP Handbook,* p. 13) combines these features to predict the difficulty (readability) of a text. Touchstone has applied the DRP readability index to a variety of popular textbooks and to common literature at all grade levels. In addition, it has measured the readability of trade publications for reading audiences of varied ages. These measures of text difficulty for particular types of text provide real-world anchors for the interpretation of student performance on the DRP.

3. Appendix E in N. Atwell, *In the Middle: New Understandings about Writing, Reading, and Learning*, 2nd ed. (Portsmouth, N.H.: Boynton/Cook, 1998).

4. Urban high school students are notoriously test averse. Knowing the standardized tests given by their districts rarely affect their academic standings or futures, they are reluctant to expend much effort on such tests. For this reason we asked the Academic Literacy teachers to encourage their students to take the DRP test seriously because it would give them good information about their own growth in reading skills over the year. We also asked the teachers to make note of students they believed to have completed the test without serious effort. The scores of 21 students (out of a total of 305) were eliminated from our findings because these students either entered the test-taking situation very late, bubbled in the answer sheet randomly, or worked for only a few minutes before putting their heads down to sleep through the remaining time. Several other students had missed one or the other testing session, so we were unable to gauge their progress. We analyzed the pre- and posttest scores of the remaining group of 216 students.